THAT'LL NEVER WORK

PORTFOLIO PENGUIN
an imprint of Penguin Canada

Published by the Penguin Group
Penguin Group (Canada), 90 Eglinton Avenue East, Suite 700, Toronto, Ontario, Canada
M4P 2Y3 (a division of Pearson Canada Inc.)

Penguin Group (USA) Inc., 375 Hudson Street, New York, New York 10014, U.S.A.
Penguin Books Ltd, 80 Strand, London WC2R 0RL, England
Penguin Ireland, 25 St Stephen's Green, Dublin 2, Ireland (a division of Penguin Books Ltd)
Penguin Group (Australia), 250 Camberwell Road, Camberwell, Victoria 3124, Australia (a division
of Pearson Australia Group Pty Ltd)
Penguin Books India Pvt Ltd, 11 Community Centre, Panchsheel Park, New Delhi – 110 017, India
Penguin Group (NZ), 67 Apollo Drive, Rosedale, Auckland 0632, New Zealand (a division of Pearson
New Zealand Ltd)
Penguin Books (South Africa) (Pty) Ltd, 24 Sturdee Avenue, Rosebank, Johannesburg 2196, South Africa

Penguin Books Ltd, Registered Offices: 80 Strand, London WC2R 0RL, England

First published 2012

1 2 3 4 5 6 7 8 9 10 (RRD)

Manufactured in the U.S.A.

Library and Archives Canada Cataloguing in Publication

    That'll never work / KPMG Enterprise.

ISBN 978-0-670-06646-9

    1. Businesspeople–Canada–Biography. 2. Business enterprises–Canada–History.
I. KPMG Enterprise (Firm) II. Title: That will never work.

HC112.5.A2T53 2012   338'.04092271   C2011-907632-2

Visit the Penguin Canada website at **www.penguin.ca**

Special and corporate bulk purchase rates available; please see **www.penguin.ca/corporatesales** or call
1-800-810-3104, ext. 2477.

ALWAYS LEARNING   PEARSON

THAT'LL NEVER WORK

BUSINESS LESSONS FROM SUCCESSFUL CANADIAN ENTREPRENEURS

KPMG ENTERPRISE

PORTFOLIO
PENGUIN

CONTENTS

FOREWORD

HAVE YOU EVER PICTURED YOURSELF AS AN ENTREPRENEUR? Wondered what it takes to start your own business? Fought to shrug off your personal doubts and join the ranks of independent business owners living the dream?

The entrepreneurs profiled in this book will entertain and enlighten you with their stories of success earned, competition burned, and lessons learned. They are also certain to make you laugh with some of their most amusing and compelling anecdotes, gleaned from their years on the front lines.

Any entrepreneur can attest to the fact that starting a business is incredibly challenging, regardless of the economic conditions. Keeping it running and growing is just as tough, if not more so. It takes commitment, conviction, intensity, a positive nature, and, as noted by each of this book's subjects, a great deal of perseverance.

But as you'll see, our Canadian entrepreneurs are resilient. They see barriers as challenges, their mistakes as learning opportunities, and they believe success is a by-product of simple hard work—not luck, destiny, or chance.

While a good idea is the genesis for almost every successful business, a good idea takes you only so far. Those who succeed typically are well plugged-in to many networks, understand their markets, create contingency plans, and react rapidly to changing economic or market realities.

But besides perseverance and the ability to adapt and evolve, entrepreneurs often require a steady hand to guide them. Most of our entrepreneurs cited the need for one or several mentors, those consultants or executives with broader business expertise. They recognized—sometimes just in time—that they needed the perspective of those who witnessed more of the ebb-and-flow nature of business. They have learned that many trials must be weathered to make it long-term. For these entrepreneurs, the experts who offered important teachings and tips have been invaluable.

For many years, KPMG Enterprise has been the guiding hand for many of Canada's most successful entrepreneurs, and we will continue to support those trying to make their mark. Helping businesses grow and succeed is our *raison d'être*. And we take great pride in the accomplishments and successes of the entrepreneurs with whom we work hand in hand.

Today, 41 per cent of all those working in the private sector are employed by companies with fewer than 50 employees. Further, 70 per cent of those working in the private sector work for companies with fewer than 500 employees. This mid-market or entrepreneurial segment currently drives about 45 per cent of the country's GDP.

Entrepreneurs spur employment, increase the business tax base, and offer services and products that have immeasurable impact on our country's economy—and our importance on a global stage. Canada's future prosperity is inextricably tied to their success.

We're quite certain you will understand why our commitment and loyalty to such entrepreneurs is so strong, as is our collective praise for their ingenuity and success. After you read these entertaining stories, we think you'll be pulling for them too.

Dennis Fortnum
Canadian Managing Partner, KPMG Enterprise

1
COMMUNITY IN THE CUP

TRACEY CLARK
Owner, Bridgehead Coffee

"The best advice I can give to people who may be starting out in business
is to have perseverance."

TRACEY CLARK

TYPE OF BUSINESS: *Retail coffee vendor* | FOUNDED: *Ottawa, Ontario, 2000*

www.bridgehead.ca

IN 1987, WHEN I TOOK A TWO-MONTH LEAVE OF ABSENCE from a kitchen management position in Ottawa to tour through northern Nicaragua, I had no idea a decade or so later I'd be at the helm of a company committed to improving the livelihood of small-scale farmers. I was pretty young and even though I was aware of Bridgehead, which was already active in my city, I hadn't really paid much attention to fair trade coffee before that trip.

It was only several years after we had started our company that I remembered what was, looking back on it, a defining moment. Travelling in the northern regions of Nicaragua—coffee country—I had been served Sanka instant coffee. I remembered thinking it was unjust that coffee farmers were so far removed from their own product. When you're young you don't really stop to consider how the different threads of your life are coming together. It's only later when you take time to reflect that you see how they all fit—and how, by taking chances along the way, you end up with a career that makes you proud.

My background is varied. In my late teens I pursued a tennis scholarship at an American university, and then returned to Canada before completing my undergraduate degree in physics, where I realized I didn't really want to be in a lab. I went to work for a group of restaurants in Ottawa for about six years, holding every position from part-time cook to chief operations officer. During that time, I honed my business skills at Newbridge Networks Corp., where I served as program director for an internal management development program. The 10-month program was like a miniature MBA course designed to help technical people become better at managing. This complemented my MBA degree from Concordia University in Montreal. My master's thesis was a little different because I focused on micro-credit. After graduating I was selected for a fellowship in international development management by the Aga Khan Foundation, which involved working with the Bangladesh Rural Advancement Committee (BRAC) in Bangladesh. BRAC was seeking to reinvigorate a diminishing sericulture industry.

Each thread is different, and yet, thankfully, it seems they all played a part in making me who I am today. I've always had an interest in social justice and development; I enjoy a business challenge; and I've always loved the instant gratification I get from being in the food industry. There's something really satisfying about serving others in a genuine way. I also feel strongly that there is a lot of room and scope for social businesses.

After returning from Nicaragua in 1987, I volunteered with Bridgehead for about a year, helping with their mail-order catalogue and fulfillment. At that time, Bridgehead had been in existence for six years. It was in the second of three incarnations, having been purchased by Oxfam Canada in 1985. The very first Bridgehead—what I often call the "founding founding"—was started in 1981 by two United Church ministers and two social activists who were concerned about the prospects of small-scale coffee farmers in Nicaragua. There was a revolutionary government in power in Nicaragua and it was under U.S. embargo. Canadians are often sympathetic to embargoed countries, and there was quite a solidarity movement in the country at that time. With that came the inauguration of Bridgehead.

The original founders decided they would import coffee beans under fair trade terms, then roast and distribute the beans across Canada to bring attention to the plight of Nicaraguan coffee farmers. It was a grassroots movement, with coffee being sold out of the backs of the founders' cars and from church basements. Their fairly traded coffee was very well received by consumers, and within three years the business outgrew its informal structure and voluntary management. The original founders approached Oxfam Canada, an international development agency, and in 1985 Oxfam agreed to buy the fledgling coffee business.

Over the following 15 years, Oxfam expanded on the original premise of Bridgehead. Oxfam transformed the company into a mail-order catalogue business, catering to its members and donors and accomplishing "development education" through alternative trade. Oxfam moved the focus of Bridgehead from coffee to handicraft, and began to work with small groups in many countries. Each year Oxfam would measure its success by how many more groups it was working with and how many more countries it had a presence in. The pinnacle for Bridgehead came under Oxfam ownership, when it had a mail-order catalogue with about 300,000 customers across the country and was working with more than 250 artisan groups in 50 countries. Its tagline was "Gifts that give twice."

My more in-depth involvement with Bridgehead started in the late 1990s. I was working as manager of the Mountain Equipment Co-op (MEC) store in Ottawa when I was approached to serve on the Bridgehead board. This came about through my earlier connection as a volunteer and with a view to my retail experience at MEC and business qualifications. At the time, the catalogue business was suffering from uncontrolled inventory issues. It was typical, as a fair trade company, to make a single order for a season, provide credit to supplier groups some six to eight months in advance of receiving products, and pay the balance upon shipping. The trouble in the pre-Internet days was that, as a mail-order catalogue business, if you didn't guess right about the product mix or numbers to order of each product, it was very easy to be left with unsold inventory. Unfortunately for Oxfam/Bridgehead, the amount of unsold inventory kept getting larger and larger and eating up critical working capital. There also was some poorly managed long-term debt that had been used to buy inventory and was coming due.

When I received my first board package, which contained the company's previous year's financial statements, it was evident to me that Bridgehead would need to restructure. I wanted to help, and at that first board meeting

I was named transition coordinator, reporting to the Bridgehead and Oxfam boards, to steer a formal restructuring. I relied on my education and professional business training to make tough decisions. The culmination of the restructuring was that Shared Interest, a Bridgehead unsecured creditor from the United Kingdom, decided to buy the company's assets. Shared Interest was considered a specialist in fair trade banking across the world and it didn't want to have a fair trade failure on its hands. Shared Interest thought I had done a good job of handling the restructuring and asked me to become managing director of the second incarnation of Bridgehead.

The goal was to turn the fair trade business around. Under the old business model, which was mainly a handicraft model, there was a mail-order catalogue and stores in Vancouver, Toronto, and Ottawa. Immediately upon taking over, we took several steps to return the company to financial health, but it became clear the business model needed to change. I proposed to the Shared Interest board that we return to Bridgehead's roots in coffee and open up coffeehouses. I looked around the country and saw that there were a lot of regional-based roasters selling fair trade coffee wholesale, but nobody was putting it into the cup.

Shared Interest simply wasn't interested. I was instructed to wind up the second incarnation of Bridgehead. If I wanted to open up a chain of coffeehouses, they told me, I could go right ahead.

By March 2000 we had wound up Bridgehead completely, which was a painful but valuable learning experience. We had to get out of leases, lay off employees, deplete unsold inventory, and find buyers for as many parts of the business as we could. The only piece we couldn't sell was the trademarked mail-order handicraft business where all of the failure had occurred.

*   *   *

Despite the misgivings of Shared Interest, I remained convinced that there was a market for fair trade coffee in the cup. Part of my initial proposal included leasing a retail outlet beside the newest Mountain Equipment Co-op store in Ottawa. Prior to flying to the United Kingdom for the board meeting, I took out an option on the lease. When Shared Interest said no, I had to consider whether I would pursue opening up a fair trade coffeehouse in this location, with or without the Bridgehead name. I felt motivated to give Bridgehead a third life and I prepared an offer for the Bridgehead trademark and presented it to Shared Interest, who told me that I had to wait until we had ensured there was no buyer for the mail-order business to which the name was attached. When there were no takers for the mail-order business, Shared Interest accepted my offer.

During the development of the coffeehouse proposal to Shared Interest I had consulted with the existing Bridgehead management team. There were 13 on the team, and only one individual, Pam Fletcher, was positive about the idea and wanted to move forward with me. The others basically said, "That will never work. You will be competing against national and international companies. The coffee market is already oversaturated. You won't be able to compete. None of us wants anything to do with it."

Even with Pam's support, and the support of my life partner, Gina, the decision wasn't easy for me. I remember the day Gina and I finally decided. We were facing three options: I had been offered a consulting role at a company in Ottawa; I had been offered a job with a start-up fair trade coffee business in Seattle; or, I could bite the bullet and take a chance on the Bridgehead coffeehouse venture. It was really exciting but also really scary. We made our decision in March of 2000 and opened our first coffeehouse in June that same year.

Having Pam on board from the start was a critical success factor. She was able to serve as a founding manager, providing the hands-on, in-store presence and freeing me up to deal with the bigger picture.

One caveat of the purchase from Shared Interest was that we would continue to operate the company according to fair trade principles. I was already aligning the business that way, but it came to me that what we were starting was really a social business. Our goal wasn't to be the next Tim Hortons or Starbucks; what we wanted to do was connect customers to farmers and be a demonstration of social and environmental sustainability for the Canadian coffee industry and beyond.

From the get-go, things went extremely well at our first location in Ottawa. We needed to make a few modifications right away—mostly minor things like adding more shelving. We also had to rethink our intention of warming food items for customers. Originally we brought in a tiny convection oven to do the job, but it soon became clear we'd need more throughput. That first year of business, 2000–2001, we did about 35 per cent better than our projections.

I often joke that my projections must have been low, but in fact there were a few reasons for our success. For starters, we were next door to the new Mountain Equipment Co-op; within a few years, the whole commercial retail area around us just blossomed and grew, bringing more traffic to the area. The store is on a traditional main street in an urban residential neighbourhood and the nearest coffee shop is a Tim Hortons nearly three kilometres away. In a way, it was an underserviced area with pent-up demand. The demographic also lined up well with what we were doing. We were in a highly educated, affluent neighbourhood.

Our initial focus was to compete against the nationals; we wanted our products to be as good as, if not better than, what they were doing, so we set our targets accordingly. Our service, our product, and the ambience of our store had to be top-notch. As much as we were concerned about serving organic and fair trade coffee, we also had to be aware that customers would judge us on other factors. Are we reasonably priced? Are they getting good service? Are we offering good value for the money? Do they like the product? A big part of our ongoing success is people's enjoyment of their experience at Bridgehead.

When it came to selecting a location for our second shop, we decided to really put our concept to the test. We chose an Ottawa neighbourhood where there were already four established coffee houses, including Starbucks, Second Cup, and Timothy's—and on top of that, we were on a side street. Opening in December 2001, that store did better in its first year than our original store. We knew we must be onto something.

At around the same time, we started to experience some logistical challenges with our food suppliers. We were working with a couple of local bakeries who were supplying home-made croissants, breads, and other really great food offerings. Some of them just weren't capable of supplying to two different locations by 6:30 A.M. Our original analysis of our competitors indicated one area of weakness was food. They all had offerings, but nothing especially appealing in terms of home-made freshness. So, we built a small kitchen into our second store and started to do some of our own morning baking.

The idea may have been born out of necessity, but right from the start our customer feedback was positive. People were impressed by our healthy, made-fresh-every-day food, and they let us know. By the time we opened our third store in July 2002, we had to relocate our kitchen to a larger premises; today, we have 30 kitchen employees making fresh food for 12 locations daily. Last year we brought our croissants in-house as well. I'm a bit of an amateur baker, so I'm proud to say we now make 6,000 croissants by hand each week. I truly believe it's a critical success factor. We're too small to ask somebody to do something special for us. We made the decision to expand the kitchen and it has served us well.

*   *   *

Despite our successes, those first few years were challenging. In 2002, I lost my mother to cancer after a two-year illness. She only got to see the plans for our third shop and expanded kitchen. The start was financially hard, too—I wasn't able to accept a salary for the first two years, just a small stipend to offset expenses. I performed some consulting contracts on the side for income. It was a really busy time, and I'm glad it's all behind me. I honestly don't know if I could do it again.

Our third shop opened on my mom's birthday, just a few months after she passed away. It was located in a rough area of town, fairly close to our second shop, so with this shop we were testing whether we had broad appeal and how close together we could locate shops. This shop was also successful from the start.

With the opening of store number four came a different challenge. Mountain Equipment Co-op, impressed by the synergy between its new Ottawa store and our first location, approached us to be in-store with them at a new power retail centre in Montreal. It was a departure from our business model and although we didn't particularly like the location—it was in the middle of an industrial park—we thought it might be a great opportunity to increase our market. To this day we call it "The store that didn't fail, but didn't succeed either." We had a great capture rate of visitors to the MEC; the problem was that there just wasn't enough MEC traffic. It turned out to be too much for us and we closed after a year.

Closing the store was like receiving a $250,000 punch in the nose very early on in our journey. We had to write off assets and there had been operating losses, so I ended up backfilling some of that with additional investment because I didn't want to burden our shareholders. We were fortunate to remove ourselves from that lease, and I credit the tough decision to my prior experience restructuring the old Bridgehead. I knew I needed to close the store quickly.

Fortunately, there was another location in Ottawa that came to our attention at around the same time. Oddly enough, we were competing with Starbucks, and the residents from the neighbourhood actually presented a petition to the landlord saying they would prefer a Bridgehead. The landlord gave the location to us, and the timing was perfect. We closed the Montreal store in May 2004 and were able to re-use the equipment and fixtures in our new store, which opened at the end of August 2004. My partner Gina gave birth to our son just a few short weeks after we closed the Montreal shop, so it was a busy time.

As of 2004 we had opened a new shop every year. We have continued at this pace and now have 12 shops, with plans for three more to open this year. Our average growth rate has been 38 per cent per year since our founding.

The best advice I can give to people who may be starting out in business is to have perseverance. You need to feed the business before you feed yourself. Have a very strong, clear picture of what it is you want to achieve and continue to build on it. Sometimes you have to be a bit "blind" in business. In retrospect, if I knew how much work would be involved, I may not have taken on the challenge of opening Bridgehead, especially when others were telling me it wouldn't work. I needed to put on my blinders in order to stay focused on my clear picture of where I wanted to be—determined and willing to take on the events at hand, like the closing of the Montreal store. To be successful in business, you need to stick to your decisions without regrets and be willing to ask for help when you need it. When we opened store number six it became clear to us that we needed to stop starving our overhead. That was a major lesson. We knew we needed to start developing a management infrastructure to carry our company forward and we had to rely on the help of others.

Gina has a background in social marketing, so it was truly a family decision to embark on the business—and, right from the beginning, she's always played a role. This has been another one of our critical success factors. Working together, side by side, to grow the business has presented its own set of challenges on a personal level. We need to balance work and family life, which isn't always easy, especially now that we have two children. When our second child arrived we both felt the strain, as neither of us was feeling we were home enough or at work enough. It's a tricky challenge to navigate, especially for two people whose identities are so wrapped up in our business.

Personal lives aside, we were somewhat naive when we were starting out. Our original business plan called for building five to seven shops in five to seven cities in five to seven years. This was too ambitious, especially because we were committed to corporate stores. We knew the corporate model would allow us to run the company according to our values and have control over our concept, but it is a capital-intensive model and requires a strong management presence. Seven stores isn't really a feasible cluster, either—it only feels like we're becoming a true cluster at a dozen stores in a city the size of Ottawa. Meanwhile, our experience in Ottawa, as well as our failed shop in Montreal, helped us realize that one shop isn't really going to cut it if we want to expand to another city. We'll need to go in with a plan to open several, ideally close together, and that requires capital. It's not out of the question, but it will be a big decision for us when the time comes.

Our future plans are to roast the coffee ourselves—in a character building in an urban area, so that the roastery can be combined with one of our coffeehouses. We also plan to expand our kitchen capabilities and open additional coffeehouses in Ottawa. We want to move to a seasonal model for our coffee and to deliver freshly roasted coffee to each of our shops daily. As a customer, you really shouldn't be served coffee 14 months past its harvest date. It just doesn't taste the same as it did at six months. And having coffee roasted so that it's as fresh as one of our baked goods would be amazing. We want to showcase just how good the coffee is from the small farmers who supply us. We believe the farmers deserve no less—and that it is quality and differentiation that will lead to sustainability for farmers in the long run.

I like to think that, in addition to helping the small-scale farmers, we're also doing some good here at home. It used to be that when I was considering a new location I would look for complementary businesses nearby already generating consumer traffic. With our last three stores we've changed that. We've gone into locations where there's virtually no traffic and put in a Bridgehead to help create a sense of neighbourhood. Watching that unfold is a real thrill for me. People like to hang out at our stores; they hold meetings, feed their babies, and there's a real community vibe. We now purposely seek out slightly larger spaces so there is more room to carry out these community functions.

We've also been able to create more opportunities for very talented employees, and I love watching them grow as individuals. While some are passionate about coffee, it's the sense of common purpose and shared values that's important. It's very special to me that I'm able to provide training for development and advancement within our company. As we've grown, we've been able to promote people and then watch them thrive as they carve out a career path with Bridgehead.

If you look around at our 200-plus employees today, every single one of them is concerned about fair trade for coffee farmers. They hold that dear. Yet I do feel there is still work to be done in terms of being a demonstration company. As we grow, I think we're in a better position to help influence customers. We want to become better at telling the story about the small-scale farmers as part of our ambition to make the connection between customers and farmers.

At the end of this fiscal year, we will have grown from $500,000 in our first year of business to nearly $15 million in annualized sales. We recently completed a customer survey indicating that 88 per cent of our customers visit our stores between four and five times a week. They're an incredibly loyal group. Many of them reported that they specifically take the time to seek us out instead of visiting a competitor. The most fulfilling answer came when we asked them what was important to them about their coffee experience and the majority mentioned our fair trade and organic commitment.

It brings me back to the memory I have from 25 years ago when I found myself drinking instant coffee during my visit to Nicaragua. Since then I have never looked back. I'm so proud of our company and our customers. It's as if the threads of my life are coming together and what's created is a weave called social responsibility.

2
PUT ON YOUR JERSEY, STICK TO THE GAME PLAN, AND BELIEVE

WAYNE RENICK, *CEO* | **ALF GARVIN,** *CFO* | **BRENT BOYLE,** *COO*
Jersey City Canada / Capz Canada

(From left) Alf Garvin, Brent Boyle and Wayne Renick

"We've built a big retail family that digs deep for each other
and gets the job done ...
We look at our staff as an extended family."

WAYNE RENICK, ALF GARVIN, BRENT BOYLE

TYPE OF BUSINESS: *Retail sports memorabilia & clothing company* | FOUNDED: *Red Deer, Alberta, 1989*

www.jerseycity.ca | www.capz.ca | www.cflshop.ca

STARTING A RETAIL CLOTHING COMPANY COMES with its share of challenges—even more so when you're young. Wayne, Alf, and Brent talk about the key factors of their success, not the least of which is "hustle," a quality they all share.

WAYNE: Today we're proud Canadians running a successful business in Canada, and it doesn't get much better than that. The products we sell bring out feelings of national pride among our customers and energize them as fans. This same pride and energy resonates throughout our company and teammates as we work together daily to be the best we can be.

Yet it has taken sweat, tears, and years of hard work to get to where we are today. We have learned how to operate a sound business, revise our plan on a daily, weekly, and yearly basis, and constantly execute it with our team. The team has always been aware of the direction we're heading, and that's one of our key success factors. Entrepreneurs are like coaches; we need to make decisions and be prepared to take calculated risks. Sometimes we stumble, but hopefully we win more than we lose.

When I reflect back to the early days of Jersey City Canada, there are two things I remember most clearly: the support and confidence I got from my parents, and being laughed out of the offices of six bankers.

I was turning 21 and fresh out of business school. I started to work part-time for Alf Garvin. Eventually I joined him full-time at the fitness club he owned at the time and at the T-shirt business we owned together. One day, Alf saw a Jersey City store in Chinook Centre in Calgary, Alberta. He learned it was a sports jersey/ memorabilia franchise, and we became sold on the idea of running one ourselves. We worked all summer to put together an amazing business plan and set out to find the capital to get our venture off the ground. We knew Jersey City was a clever brand and we wanted to be a part of it. My own personal goal was to learn the business and operate a successful store. I was interested in business and sports so Jersey City seemed to be a business that would combine the best of both worlds. I just put on my running shoes and went for it.

From what I recollect, one of our first negotiations was with my parents, who were happy to loan me $15,000 of their hard-earned money to help us get started. My parents have always been very supportive, and even though this was a risky, unproven venture, they stepped up with a loan. My dad ensured that one of my first lessons in business was to pay them back the principal plus an agreed-upon interest rate, which I proudly did.

Meanwhile, our experience with lenders was the exact opposite. I remember a banker telling us we didn't have proper financials, to which Alf and I replied, "Turn to page seven of our business plan." Then he said we didn't have proper customer demographic studies, and we told him to turn to page 19. It went on like that for a while; it was obvious the banks weren't taking us seriously and weren't willing to take a risk on us. Thankfully, we were pretty stubborn guys who never gave up.

ALF: We had a lot of people in the beginning who did not believe in us. The important thing was that we believed in ourselves. By the time we'd gone through six different lenders, two of whom wouldn't even look at our proposal, we were a little bit tired. Not only was retail somewhat frowned upon 22 years ago, but Wayne was 21 and I was going on 27. The lenders kind of looked sideways at us. Six lenders turned us down before we went to the Alberta Opportunity Company for the second time. With the support of other people in the industry who vouched for us, we were able to get them to lend us the money. Without this perseverance, I don't think we would have gotten started.

Like Wayne, I also consider myself lucky to have parents who believed in me. They remortgaged their house to lend me $25,000. They've always been extremely supportive and trusting of my abilities and work ethic. I was already in the fitness and T-shirt business but my goal was to continue working for myself, earn a good living, and positively influence the people around me.

It was 1989—the year the Calgary Flames won the Stanley Cup—when we were finally successful in financing our first Jersey City franchise at the Bower Place shopping centre in Red Deer, Alberta.

BRENT: My foray into Jersey City started out a bit differently. Early on my parents had taught me the value of a strong work ethic, so rather than borrowing money and starting off with a franchise like Wayne and Alf, I invested what I could as an employee—a lot of "sweat equity"—into the business. It was fall of 1990 and I had a career writing speeches for the government. When we lost the election, I was looking for work and found myself at a Jersey City store in Regina. I had always been involved in sports. I had worked in retail as a kid and while working my way through university, so it was something that appealed to me. Ironically, one of the predictions in my high school yearbook was that I would run a Saskatchewan Roughriders memorabilia store some day because the Riders and business were all I talked about.

I worked at the store for two to three years at a very modest wage, learning the operational ropes and fine-tuning my management skills. Eventually my sweat equity paid off and I was afforded the opportunity to acquire shares with the assistance of Clare Seal, my former business partner. Clare was the guy who gave me the chance to be involved with Jersey City—something I believed I earned but that he didn't necessarily have to offer. I am thankful he gave me that opportunity. When we needed capital to expand our Regina business, I turned to family for financing. My cousin and his wife (Murray and Val Nunns) and my wife's uncle and aunt (Dave and Lois Weick) took a chance and invested in me and my young family—without much of a business plan presentation, I might add. One of my proudest moments early on in my business life came when I paid those loans back in full.

By the time Alf and Wayne made their move to acquire the Jersey City banner from The Forzani Group Ltd. several years later, I was part owner of two Jersey City franchise locations and an e-commerce business in Regina. I had met Alf and Wayne on numerous occasions at franchise meetings and we knew we had similar ideas about where our individual locations could and should go. Whereas their strength was on the process side and understanding the systems needed to run multiple locations, my strength was being hands-on in the day-to-day operations of the stores, and I learned some valuable lessons there.

ALF: Timing was everything. Wayne and I launched our first Jersey City store in Red Deer at the beginning of a very good retail season. Within our first year we actually made a profit. Within nine months we purchased our second store and within 15 months we had a third. Our growth was quick and we soon realized we needed to develop systems and processes and start delegating tasks if we were going to succeed. Wayne became our buyer because he was good with the business and fashion sense, while I jumped into finance and information technology (IT). I didn't have specific training in the area; you might say I just learned from the school of hard knocks. Our goal was to expand the business so we could increase our salaries, becoming macromanagers as opposed to micromanagers. We believed in our game plan and we stayed focused on our goals.

Still, when we first bought the franchise we expected it to be like McDonald's. We figured we'd receive support and that our franchisor, The Forzani Group, would provide a winning formula. That wasn't the case. Forzani was in the infant stages of franchising and was feeling its way as it went.

So, right from our first year in, we knew we had to put our hands into it and put our own signature on the business. Both Wayne and I served on the franchise committee for several years and were directly involved with our franchisor on a regular basis. We were in their office, in their face, trying to get the support we needed, and we didn't take no for an answer. I would say probably 70 to 75 per cent of the initiatives came from the franchisees. It wasn't very often the franchisor would come to us explaining how things were going to be done.

WAYNE: In the beginning, Alf and I were told to "go hang out for a couple of days in the Chinook store." That was the extent of our training. We spent a day there but by noon the second day we said, "Okay, time to leave." Here we were, peppering the staff with a hundred questions an hour and they didn't have the answers. It wasn't a traditional franchise. For a $25,000 franchise fee you got a cool store concept and a link to some suppliers who handled some unique products. That was about it.

For the first five years, there was no real marketing plan from the franchisor. You have to remember that between us—Brent included—we had five of the first franchise locations. As the franchise grew over the next eight years or so across Canada, there was more infrastructure in place at the franchisor level. But early on, it was a work in progress. Most of us were successful because people knew the name Jersey City, especially in the West. The corporate advertising contribution basically amounted to in-store signage and flyers.

There was no system—no proven formula—so it was easy for guys to over-order and wind up in a bad cash-flow position. You could order thousands of hockey jerseys, but then you'd be on the hook for them if they didn't sell. Without a strong business model, you had to battle through it; you had to learn on your feet.

BRENT: The pitch from the franchisor consisted of a promise that new franchisees would get a mall location to drive traffic along with a cool store concept; that was the extent of the corporate marketing campaign. Success actually hinged on the levels of energy and passion of each individual.

As the franchise grew, there wasn't a lot of operational support, and, moving forward, it was easy to spin your company into trouble if you were given too much leeway on critical business decisions—which, unfortunately, many did.

We were paying royalties and receiving less and less, or so it seemed. And there wasn't much to start with. That's when Wayne and Alf really started to go after Forzani to see what they could do to take the brand over. It's also when my partner and I agreed to help. It was a matter of self-preservation. We were already doing most of the business ourselves, so why not take over?

WAYNE: Also, around 1996 or 1997, Forzani Group was experiencing a lot of difficulties. Their stock price was under pressure and the business was performing below expectations. There were hockey lockouts, labour unrest, a baseball strike, and declining sales across the Jersey City chain. A lot of the franchisees started to lose control of their businesses and many went bankrupt.

It was nerve-racking. Most businesses were amalgamating and getting larger and here we were trying to buy a piece of a business from a larger parent company. Our favourite story is derived from a meeting with the CEO of the Forzani Group. He said, "The banks don't want you; the landlords don't want you; the customers don't want you; and the vendors don't want you." We looked up at him, slapped a loonie down on his desk and said, "Great. We'll take the business."

Of course, we paid a little bit more than a loonie, but six months later we hammered out a deal to buy the Jersey City name and trademark from The Forzani Group. It was 1999 and together we had seven Jersey City store locations.

Our first order of business was to revamp everything, from finance to IT. We formed new relationships with our vendors, bought a new head office, broadened our relationships with landlords, and essentially started from scratch.

ALF: Existing franchisees were invited to come along with the purchase and to help us take the company in a new direction. But even they scoffed at our idea. Since we were purchasing the name, we gave them two years: they either had to pick a time to come on board or change their name. At that point, I think, arrogance got in the way for some of them.

WAYNE: It was a very different group. A lot of the franchisees weren't business people; they were guys who loved sports. Perhaps they didn't believe in our game plan. And, to be honest, there weren't a lot of franchisees left. Many of them had gone bankrupt. The high-water mark under Forzani Group was about 34 stores, and by 1999 it had been whittled down to 11.

From then on, we went from being a scattered franchise to being a wholly owned corporation with five partners (today we have three). It was easier to control our company and we brought in new staff, both internal and external candidates, and put them into specialized positions.

Part of the key to our success was having the wherewithal to delegate key positions to teammates who were better at those job functions than we were—like our director of purchasing, Len Stener, a 15-year teammate. It freed us up to plan the business while they had the freedom to do what they did best. Everything I had just learned at business school (law, finance, marketing, HR) suddenly was put into the real-life situations that were coming at us all at once. It was challenging but fun!

At the same time, sports became more prevalent in Western Canada. We had a lot of different teams, whether it was the Edmonton Oilers and Calgary Flames in the National Hockey League or the Calgary Stampeders and Saskatchewan Roughriders in the Canadian Football League. Even Major League Baseball was growing in popularity.

We started to market our company more aggressively and sent consumers the targeted message that Jersey City is the place to go for licensed sports products. We also built relationships with the NHL, CFL, NFL, NBA, Team Canada, and Major League Baseball. Today we've become a very important retail channel for suppliers like Reebok, CCM, Nike, and New Era. We pump a lot of pride out the door to sports fans.

In the early days we went to a lot of seminars and brought in consultants to guide us. We have always surrounded ourselves with the right people. One of our key success factors is seeking advice, analyzing it, and then making the proper strategic decisions. At the end of the day you have to believe in yourself, believe in your team, and make things happen.

An example of this came when we were looking to extend our headwear business in 2004. We decided we wanted to start a new fashion headwear concept and name it Capz, Canada's Hottest Headwear. We went to a fashion trade show with a totally different supplier base than our Jersey City business. Normally when we attend a licensed trade show, we have reps running out to talk to us because of our buying power. At this branded trade show, we would stand at the booths and no one would let us in. I won't name names, but they simply wouldn't give us the time of day—and, looking back, our new concept could easily have died right there.

So we ended up starting out with piecemeal brands, persisting year after year to build the Capz brand within our stores, one supplier at a time. It's ironic, but a lot of those brands that wouldn't let us in their booths back in 2004 are now fully engaged with us, actually marketing and doing promotions within our Capz stores, which makes us proud.

We're also proud of our on-line business. In 2009 we partnered with Team Canada, and today we're the exclusive on-line retail partner for the CFL. In fact, we have three e-commerce sites: www.jerseycity.ca, www.capz.ca, and www.CFLshop.ca.

As owners, we're right in the fire and sometimes it's easy to lose sight of what we've built. For me, the thrill comes from knowing that we've gone from one store to 27 Jersey City stores, 7 Capz stores, and 3 e-commerce sites.

I can still hear my mom saying, "Are you sure you need another store?" I can also remember the day I tried to get my first job at three different sports stores in Red Deer and was told they weren't hiring. Since then I have gotten to know the individual owners. One store has closed, one has remained the same, and one has changed his store concept. Our drive to succeed has translated into long-standing success, and for that we are extremely thankful.

We have built our company into the largest independent licensed retailer in Canada, and we've done that while maintaining our profitability, our industry relationships, and, most importantly, our integrity within our team. As a company we have a lot to be proud of, whether it's the three of us or all 295 of us.

BRENT: I think we've had a couple of defining moments over the years. One was during the NHL lockout in 2004–2005. Instead of looking for different things to do, we chose to get better at what we already did. We refined our systems and looked for better ways to distribute product. We looked at better ways to purchase and better banking arrangements, and went the whole nine yards. Rather than focus our efforts on finding a new revenue stream, we figured out how to improve existing aspects of our business.

So, during the lockout, our NFL and CFL business grew exponentially, and it stayed that way even after the NHL came back.

Another defining moment happened about four years ago. Wayne was involved in a very serious accident and we called our team into the boardroom. I remember this as if it were yesterday. We were opening a store in Winnipeg and I had to fly back to share the news that Wayne was hurt and we weren't sure when—or if—he would be back. It was then we had an epiphany; we realized just how skilful our team was and how much we could lean on them to bring more to the table when times were tough. We didn't even have to ask them to step up. It just happened.

From that moment on, we, as owners, stopped wearing so many hats. We now have a lot of talented people who share our passion for the business. We've built a big retail family that digs deep for each other and gets the job done—and our company has been different since that day.

ALF: Brent and Wayne take the macro look at business and I tend to get more detailed. But among the three of us, we deal with everybody on a somewhat personal level and it's worked out very well. We're approachable. We look at our staff as an extended family. People know they can come to us with work and, if necessary, personal challenges. One of the most important things we received early on was the support from our families so now we're trying to reciprocate, giving back to our people and our communities.

Most recently, we've raised more than $175,000 to provide 22 wishes for the Make-A-Wish Foundation here in Alberta. This type of effort just reminds us of how fortunate we are. Sure, we've worked hard, but when we see some of the misfortune of others, it makes a big difference to know we're able to help, even if it's only to give them a few weeks away from the stress of their lives.

WAYNE: About 10 years ago we came up with a vision and a mission statement for our company based on working hard and playing hard. There are a lot of fun things that we do—from Fun Fridays, where we get together to try something new as a group, to our managers' meetings, which have turned into a challenge cup between territories. We have a good bonus structure, so if the company is successful, our employees share in the success. We also hold in-store contests for our staff to win prizes, including trips to Grey Cup, All-Star, or NFL football games. I've always said smart choices equal smart results. As a team, I think we've brought this saying to life.

BRENT: One of my favourite sayings comes from former UCLA Coach John Wooden, who said, "Hustle makes up for many mistakes." That probably defines our company as a whole. When there's a need or a tight deadline, everybody just rolls up their sleeves and gets the job done—whether it falls under their job description or not. That's our culture. Everybody hustles to make stuff happen. In business it's always good to learn from mistakes, but if you spend too much time looking backwards, you're going to miss what's coming ahead. From the day we started Jersey City Canada, our success has been about the little things dear to people's hearts. Despite the fact that retail doesn't have a proud history of staff retention, we have a relatively large group who have received five-year rings, as well as four or five employees we've sent to the Pro Bowl in Hawaii to honour their 10-year anniversaries.

Many of our employees are either directly involved in sport or huge sports fans, which allows for us to offer a lot of unique experiences with natural tie-ins. Our goal is to create an atmosphere where work is more than just a paycheque. Retail doesn't pay a glamorous wage so we try to keep employees interested in other ways. When we hold a managers' challenge cup, we try to find a unique sport no one has tried. This year we battled it out on a sledge hockey rink.

We strive to always take on new challenges, not just during special events, and sometimes we must act without checking every possible angle and without getting unanimous agreement from those on the outside. If you believe in your passion and your work ethic, you can make a lot of things happen.

ALF: When someone tells you something will never work, the best approach is to do your research and analyze whether what they're saying is valid. Then be honest with yourself. I'd like people to be able to look back at us one day and say, "Gee, those guys worked hard. They ran an honest company. They were great to their people and they made a difference in the community." I think if Wayne and I hadn't been honest with ourselves and hadn't believed in what we were doing, we may have listened to that sixth banker and we wouldn't be here today. We would have returned the money to our parents and maybe thought of doing something different. People didn't take us seriously, but 22 years later we're still here!

If you come to the conclusion that the naysayers are wrong, believe in yourself, in your work, and in your product, and most of all hustle and never give up, you won't be disappointed!

3

A SWING, A MISS, AND FINALLY—AN INVESTMENT BUSINESS HOME RUN

CHARLIE SPIRING

Senior Investment Advisor & Vice-Chair & Director of NBF Wealth Management
Former Chairman & CEO, Wellington West Holdings Inc.

"With the right attitude, you will almost always succeed in business."

CHARLIE SPIRING

TYPE OF BUSINESS: *Investment management firm* | FOUNDED: *Winnipeg, Manitoba, 1993*

www.wellwest.ca

THERE'S A REASON WHY I VIVIDLY RECALL THE TORONTO BLUE JAYS' back-to-back World Series wins in 1992 and 1993—and Joe Carter's game-winning home run in the bottom of the ninth inning of game six in '93 is only part of it.

The second series stands out in my mind because during that time I was embroiled in a competitive battle of my own. I was slugging it out as an investment dealer, trying to launch an innovative investment business. Just like Carter and the Jays, I also hit one way out of the park, and both of these moments represent cherished memories.

The idea for Wellington West came to me in the fall of 1992 while I was working at Midland Walwyn in Winnipeg. In my arrogance, I thought that if I was a top broker, my clients should receive the best treatment and they should get the best value.

My idea was to create an independent investment firm that offered customized solutions to clients, using a firm like Midland Walwyn to handle all the back-office activities. I wanted to spend less time on producing statements, contracts, and settlements, and focus more on adding value for clients: stock selection, portfolio balancing, comprehensive performance returns and more meaningful reporting—services to make a client's life easier.

My ultimate goal was to create a lot of enterprise value. In our industry, if you generate good, recurring revenue, you enhance the client experience and at the same time create your own book of business that, in theory, you can sell someday for good value. At the time, we were creating significant enterprise value and just exporting it to the banks and brokerage firms. I felt I wasn't getting my share of the enterprise value that I was building and that there had to be a better way. I thought I could create more value for my clients and for myself by offering customized investment solutions, which would bring higher returns to my clients and in turn be more profitable for us.

Rather than sneaking off in the middle of the night with my box of client files under my arm, I approached Midland Walwyn's board of directors with an idea: if they would allow me to create an independent arm for customized investments and agree to handle the back-office details, we could build a win–win model for servicing top brokers across the country. They actually thought the idea was rather brilliant, and in hindsight it turned out to be more brilliant than even I understood. We negotiated a contract, and after a lot of back and forth we finally agreed that Wellington West Capital Inc. would open on April 1, 1993.

Midland Walwyn would remain my back office and be connected through capital market producer supply and a full offering of interest-bearing bonds, but I would remain an independent firm. I called it my "umbilical cord" to the outside world of investments. As it turned out, nothing was as easy as it first appeared. The process of gaining regulatory approval was not as easy as anticipated. In fact, it was slow and painful, but I guess that's part of life.

The relationship with Midland Walwyn did not last and my "umbilical cord" was cut just as I was getting started. It took me until October 1993 to officially cut all ties to my former employer and become truly independent. Just as game six of the World Series happened that second year, I realized my dream. I am very proud that we were profitable from day one. Out of respect for Midland Walwyn, I signed a two-year non-compete agreement to not impair their business. Any client who didn't want to follow me could stay at Midland Walwyn.

For the first six years, Wellington West exploded onto the scene. Five other Midland Walwyn employees decided to come with me to start the company and we used TD Securities as our back office. We doubled our business overnight. There are always little challenges you come across in the beginning, but we had really smart people who worked hard. That's the Winnipeg way. If there's a problem, we deal with it, fix it, and press on. Our entire group had this "get it done" attitude that took every challenge and turned it into an opportunity for us.

Initially, we dealt with a slightly higher net worth demographic in the marketplace. These clients' needs are the same as a person with very small amounts of money to invest, but they are willing to pay a bit more because they really prefer the complete solution when it comes to their investing needs. They like to go to a one-stop shop where we can direct all of their assets, find them a better place to invest, and report in a way that's easy to understand. In short, I had figured out how we could customize investments, do it effectively, and in the process add value for Wellington. We were beating the biggest and best people at their own game. I was using TD Bank as a nice, safe place to hold assets while I was customizing solutions for my clients at the front office. My clients knew their assets were safe, and they knew they were getting more.

My next greatest decision driving our first year in business was to offer the other five employees who started with me the opportunity to buy in as partners. We were so successful that they were paid back their investment in about a year's time. This made me appreciate the importance of employee ownership. We offered Wellington shares to all employees and, as time went on, more than 90 per cent of our staff became shareholders. By June of 2011, almost all of our more than 650 employees held Wellington shares. This was an incredibly high take-up, but again, one of the secret sauces in our success was that we had unbelievably good people who believed in us. Our shareholders were all committed to the cause. We had more than 50 branches across Canada and every branch loved the concept of being a shareholder.

For eight years, we operated as what I call a "one-shop wonder" in Winnipeg. In 1999, we switched our back office from TD Securities to National Bank, as it was regarded as more of a full-service back office and it had really stepped up the quality of its offerings for clients. It was painful to make the change, but it was the best move for our clients' long-term interests.

Around that same time I got the idea to replicate Winnipeg. I got on my pony and went to Saskatoon, Moose Jaw, Red Deer, and Regina. While jokingly calling ourselves the "Western Wonder," we went to the smaller towns and cities that Bay Street did not care to visit and asked honest, hard-working people with their own brand and franchise to join our dynamic culture. It was hard to find them, but once we did they loved our idea of shared ownership and quickly joined forces.

Not everyone in our industry is an entrepreneur, so we had to dig deep to find potential partners. In smaller towns you tend to find investment dealers who are ignored by the larger head offices. Head-office guys might actually fly over them in their private jets, but they would never stop in Moose Jaw or Saskatoon. That was our joke to break the ice: See that plane? That's your boss, flying first class.

We also got a little bit lucky because CI Fund Management Inc. had decided to buy Assante Corp., and when they left Winnipeg they left a lot of well-trained, smart, honest, and hard-working partners behind. We were able to hand-pick those we wanted to join us. Then Richardson Securities left Winnipeg, which opened up another talent pool. All of a sudden, we went from being the second biggest independent investment dealer in Winnipeg to being *the* independent.

From the start, our business plan was to be under market in the four big centres in Canada and to be over market in every smaller city across our great country. The giants out East are so eastern-centric they forget a dollar in Saskatoon is the same as a dollar in Toronto. There may be more corporate depth in Toronto, but there's also more competition. Dealing from Winnipeg, we had humble roots and people easily connected to us. Another advantage was that we were the geographic centre of North America. A visit to the east or west coast was a three-hour trip. I could fly out of Winnipeg at 7 A.M., have my first meeting in Vancouver at 8:30 A.M., and catch a 6 P.M. flight back to be home before midnight.

Our batting average was also high. As an independent firm we needed to compete with banks and broker-ages with multi-billion-dollar assets behind them. There's something in Canada called a "bought deal," where investors will buy into a deal before it closes, assuming the risk of the deal. There's many a day I'd wake up in the morning at 6:30 and my first call would be from my capital markets guy who wanted to do a bought deal. Our maximum was about $100 million. Sometimes we'd put $100 million out there on one deal—it could be for a nanosecond or as long as two weeks—which meant we were essentially risking a great deal of the firm's capital. For the banks, $100 million is nothing.

Those are the times when your cheeks pucker a little when you think of the risk, and you know you can't afford to be wrong. Fortunately, our firm was right 99.9 per cent of the time, where our competitors may have been right 60 per cent of the time. My own theory is that when you give people too much capital to work with, they sometimes take bad risks. We had limited capital and limited resources, but we continued to fight way above our weight class. It's because we had to be more efficient with our capital, our resources—and, for that matter, with everything. It was our money out there and we needed to get it right most of the time.

Our market awareness, or market sense, was near perfect. There were world events beyond our control tugging at and impacting our deals, but we handled this with a rock-solid balance sheet. In 2008, we were ready to take Wellington public but we could see the financial world wasn't as strong as it had been. We decided to wait. In fact, we wanted to make sure we had a strong balance sheet so we sold 12.5 per cent of our firm to our back-office provider, National Bank. This not only gave us more capital to work with, but also turned out to be one of the most brilliant things we could have done. A couple of months later we were in the middle of the worst recession of my career, yet there we were with this great balance sheet. Meanwhile, we watched as Merrill Lynch, Bear Stearns, and Lehman Brothers were pulled underwater by heavy debt and toxic assets. Watching them disappear, I was reminded again of the kind of firm I wanted to create. When you're nimble and quick, as we were, the "ball field" can be an amazing place to play.

This is a great lesson for most entrepreneurs: Always give yourself more room in your balance sheet than you think it's going to take.

Most entrepreneurs tend to underestimate how long it takes to bring a product to market, while overestimating revenue. You need to be realistic with your projections and you need to maintain a solid balance sheet so you're ready for surprises.

One of the greatest lessons in history came from Bill Gates. Today, most people think of him as the richest man in the world, but there was a time when he was a small business owner and his biggest client didn't pay him for eight or nine months. He actually came within two or three months of not making it. Bill Gates now keeps a hoard of cash on hand. He learned a lot from the scary balance sheet and he got through it. However, he came close to disaster in the beginning. Can you imagine the world being rewritten without Microsoft?

Another lesson: You can't operate in neutral.

You've either got your foot on the accelerator or you're going backwards. You have to have an adaptive instinct to keep moving ahead in business, to create innovative products, and to keep finding new things. That was another great skill of our team at Wellington. We listened when our customers asked for something new, for variations on our offerings, or for other ways of achieving goals. We'd often take a financial product from another country and re-engineer it for the Canadian market. A lot of times, our successes were born out of sheer market sense. We also relied on the expertise of Meir Statman, an accomplished researcher and expert in behavioural finance who served as a trusted adviser to our firm.

One deal I'm particularly proud of came about when the government decided to privatize Manitoba Telephone System in 1996. We were a pretty small business at the time, but I knew privatizations were generally priced below market. We had a priority right to buy in Manitoba before the rest of Canada. Because we knew the rest of Canada would want to buy it after us, we fought like dogs to let everyone know they should buy this stock.

We had a phone line set up here—925-4MTS—and soon everyone thought we were the lead underwriter. We raised $100 million on the underwriting and it was at $13 per share. When it went to $50 we made a lot of money as a firm, but more importantly—and this is a great source of pride for me—our clients made a lot of money.

This type of deal provided the biggest rush for me at Wellington. I love seeking out a risk for return on a level that would make Las Vegas jealous. With privatizations anywhere in the world, you'll typically have a better business when it's run by business executives. I had studied privatizations for years and here was one we could do with our very own team. It was another example of the benefit of a home-field advantage. We took a full swing and it was another home run.

We also became a leader in buying bonds at better rates for our clients. One day I dreamed up this idea of re-insuring bonds. At the time, Government of Canada bonds were paying 6 to 7 per cent and corporate bonds were paying 11 to 13 per cent. The spread was too wide. I tried to figure out how to provide something supported by the safety net of the government but with the higher return of the corporate offering.

Not only did I come up with an idea, I did something no one else in the investment world was prepared to do. I picked up the phone and called the CEO of Lloyd's. My idea was that Lloyd's should insure bonds. Using the Lloyd's triple-A balance sheet as security, it could insure a single, double, or triple-B bond, charge a 2 to 3 per cent fee to guarantee it, and come out ahead. By restructuring Canadian bonds this way, we were able to get our clients a 9 per cent return on what would have been a 6 per cent bond.

When I called the CEO of Lloyd's, he liked the idea right away and told me to fly over on Tuesday and meet him for breakfast on Wednesday. His sales team took me golfing and then to dinner; by the end of Wednesday night, I said "Do we have a deal?" I'll never forget his reply: "Yes. We had a deal this morning. We just wanted to see what kind of character you were." They took my idea a hundred thousand degrees further and made a lot of money at it. It was fantastic for both Lloyd's and Wellington. We took advantage of those bonds for a while, giving our clients no more risk than a government bond at a 50 per cent higher return. Our brokers were happy, our clients were happy, Lloyd's was happy—it all worked out well. Eventually, the margins got too thin so we walked away from it, but at the time it significantly contributed to our growth.

Those were magical points in our business. We also had our challenges. Early on, we were short on horse-power at the top. I was writing a book, running a business, and overseeing capital markets. It was too much work for a 16-hour day and I was killing myself. A lot of small businesses can't afford to bring on help, so you end up doing it yourself. We had to stop, reflect for a moment, and bite the bullet, bringing in some professional accounting, capital markets, and operations people. It's really important in business to look around the corner so you can cut in ahead of potential problems.

Sometimes people are afraid to admit someone knows more than they do. Not me. I realize a lot of people out there are much smarter than I am—not to mention better looking and taller—and I find that their services are available for the asking. There's a lot of great thought leadership out there, but I don't have to own it. I simply pay for the services when I really need them. I have a professional lawyer, insurance agent, and travel agent, and they're all better at those things than I am. I don't aspire to be the best travel agent in the world; I simply want to get on a plane and fly and know I've received good value. Sometimes you have to learn to let go.

Another lesson someone in my business finds out early is that when the Americans get the flu, Canadians get a cold. We can't avoid their problems, no matter how cautious and careful Canadian investors tend to be. In 2008, our banks' share prices dropped more than 50 per cent. Everybody owns a piece of the decline—whether through pension plans, mutual funds, or directly—so it has a huge effect. It was a great time to figure out whether to buy more bank stock, hold on to it, or sell. A tonne of mistakes were made during this time, but I'm proud to say our firm avoided most of them. This is partly because I'm a "bear market baby" at heart. I started out in this business in 1981 when the market was awful and you had to learn how to survive in bad times—how to pick through to find good opportunities and good stocks. This training paid off big time for our firm in the fall of 2008. My biggest changes and my best moves for my clients typically happen during bad times, when good stuff goes on sale and people tend to lose their cool. I love the market action. The world's problems are my problems. Every morning I wake up to what has happened overnight and it's my job to dissect it. When the market opens at 8:30 A.M., people here want to know what's going on.

At Wellington, we had a different mindset than most investment dealers. We actually applauded people for making mistakes—as long as they were new ones. We gave people some freedom to be creative. This encouraged them to look under rocks and everywhere else for the next great opportunity, knowing it was okay to go after a few bad ones.

The other thing I love about what I do is getting the opportunity to tell our story. Most CEOs don't maintain a retail practice anymore and most don't enjoy talking to brokers. I still do. I love it. I'm out there in the field every day. Brokers may be a pain—they're egotistical, they're arrogant, and they're demanding—but I'm one of them. I connect better with brokers than with most people. Today, when I am not serving my clients I'm on the road, staying mobile and recruiting people who are unhappy somewhere else.

I think that with the right attitude, you will almost always succeed in business. Back in 1993, a lot of people doubted the Toronto Blue Jays' ability to win back-to-back titles, just as a lot of people doubted me. When I was opening Wellington, my own lawyer pulled me aside to tell me I was the dumbest man on Earth. He just didn't get it. But that was okay—because, thankfully, a lot of other people did "get it." And I couldn't have done it without them. I am so grateful to the people who joined me along the way to build this great business. And to our great clients for allowing us to serve them. Our achievement was further validated in the summer of 2011 when National Bank agreed to acquire our company for $333 million. This was a really proud moment for me. We had really done it—we made it to the big leagues! And we're not finished yet. I am excited as we embark on this next chapter in our history. As we join forces with National Bank, we leverage both the strength of a forward-thinking bank and our unique culture. We truly believe that National Bank affords us the best opportunity to realize our dream of becoming the number-one wealth management firm in the country.

When someone tells you you're crazy, it helps to build a moat around the island of your business. Others won't venture into your territory because it doesn't make any sense to them. Even today, most of my competitors will stop when someone says, "That won't work." But if you're willing to go the extra mile, to figure out how to build a bridge across the river, victory isn't only within reach … it can be yours.

4
PASSION PLUS MISSION

Moving from Aid to Trade

BARB STEGEMANN

The 7 Virtues Beauty Inc. / The 7 Virtues Communications Group

"If you make a mistake in your business, it's got to be fixed, one hundredfold. The customer must be wowed into making that 180-degree turn in their impression of your company."

BARB STEGEMANN

TYPE OF BUSINESS: *Perfume, professional speaker* | FOUNDED: *Halifax, Nova Scotia, 2008, 2010*

www.the7virtues.com

I AM AN INCREDIBLY GRATEFUL CANADIAN. Though I have humble roots, this country of opportunity has allowed me to grow into a university-educated woman with two successful companies. Not many countries in the world offer all their citizens the chance to experiment with learning and personal pursuits without judgment or punishment for expressing themselves. In the same way Canada has unlocked possibilities for me, I feel it is our responsibility to swing open the doors to the banquet and allow others to rise to their potential through economic empowerment.

I've worn a few hats in my career. I have been a journalist and a consultant. I have even run for the nomination to serve in public office. In 2008, I wrote a book of personal philosophy and began making my living mostly as an author and public speaker.

However, a couple of years ago I felt compelled to start up a perfume business. The inspiration came from my long-time best friend and mentor, Captain Trevor Greene, who very nearly died on a peacekeeping mission in Afghanistan in 2006.

Trevor was in a small community called Shinkay, sitting with his fellow peacekeepers and the village elders, discussing how to bring clean drinking water, education, and health care to the women and children. Suddenly he was attacked from behind, struck by the axe of a 16-year-old Taliban man who didn't want the people in his community to have free will—or even free thought. The man partially split Trevor's brain with that one awful swing before Trevor's fellow soldier shot and killed him. It is a miracle my friend survived. As you can imagine, the road he has travelled since then has been tremendously challenging.

I realize that starting a company may not be a typical response to a friend's horrible tragedy. After it happened, though, I was looking for ways to support his mission, part of which includes liberating Afghan families from terrorism.

I wanted to prove to the people of Afghanistan that they weren't alone and we were going to shine light on what was beautiful. I also wanted to show my best friend Trevor that his mission wasn't in vain; there are many of us who care deeply about freedom, literacy, and economic empowerment.

I dedicated my 2008 book, *The 7 Virtues of a Philosopher Queen*, to Trevor. Then, during speaking engagements, I found that I would talk about him and get a common response. Canadians would say, "When it comes to Afghanistan our hands are tied. As civilians, what can we do? How can we make a difference? How can we effect change?" I began to realize there aren't many ways, outside of charity, for citizens to be a part of the process of ending strife and war. To make real change, you either have to be a soldier or a world leader.

One day I read an article about a gentleman named Abdullah Arsala, who was employing more than 2,500 farmers in his community to grow legal crops in Afghanistan as an alternative to the poppy crop. Since the illegal poppy crop represents the base for about 90 per cent of the world's heroin, and that heroin is on our own city streets, it's in our interest to care.

On the subject of Afghanistan we've been asking the wrong questions. Instead of "Should we be there?" we should be asking, "How should we be there?" When I read the article about legal crops, I saw how I should be there.

So my book was the foundation and the fragrance is the thesis brought to life. We must flex our buying power in new ways to make positive and impactful changes.

Things started moving quickly. I travelled to Ottawa to meet with some executives from CIDA who told me I would need to find and speak to Abdullah Arsala directly. They connected me with the right non-governmental organization (NGO) to meet with the ambassador to Afghanistan, soon finding Abdullah and making a deal to buy orange blossom oils through his company, Gulestan. I chose a perfumer and we soon had one thousand bottles of our perfume produced and delivered to my garage. The 7 Virtues Beauty Inc. was born.

We launched just after that in Toronto, Ottawa, and Halifax. My friends threw perfume parties to give my product more exposure, and I stayed on their couches for the promotional tour. Fortunately, we got a lot of media coverage. I decided to take my business idea to the CBC TV reality show *Dragons' Den*. It was one of the best decisions of my life.

Of the five thousand Canadian companies auditioning to be on *Dragons' Den*, 300 make it. Only 20 of those 300 get deals on air that ultimately pass due diligence. Mine was one of them. When I got accepted by three of the Dragons, I chose to go with investor W. Brett Wilson.

He was a perfect fit. Within the first 48 hours he had me booked in front of some Young Presidents' Organization (YPO) audiences. I had asked on the show for his wisdom and counsel and he jumped on board. He has helped in so many ways. We've even done an in-store blitz at The Bay together.

Three months after we'd passed our due diligence with Brett I cold-called The Bay. In just 10 minutes they responded and agreed to sell my perfume in 91 Canadian stores. And they pay me in 30 days, unlike most suppliers, whose products are sold on consignment.

It was the start of a terrific relationship. They even helped us design the stands for our perfume. They're easy to work with but, more than that, they took a chance on us. They continue to mentor me because they feel this is a great Canadian success story.

Our goal is to encourage others, especially women, to trade with businesspeople in Afghanistan, Haiti, and other nations experiencing strife as part of the solution to building peace. The 7 Virtues Beauty Inc. does this by trying to empower women at the beauty counter. My book, sold alongside the perfume, is designed to encourage women to empower themselves by using their buying power and natural, often untapped, abilities.

I took all the Stoic texts that I've been moved by, including Marcus Aurelius, Sir Winston Churchill, Mary Wollstonecraft, Simone de Beauvoir, Adam Smith, and Plato, and I cobbled together a book for women. I took the four stoic virtues that Churchill and the boys used when they were going through war and strife—truth, courage, justice, wisdom—and I added three more: wonder, moderation, and beauty.

I want young women at the beauty counter to find my book and realize that they have enormous buying power—enough to effect world change—and that their beauty represents their inner strength and dignity. I want them to be empowered.

Unfortunately, not everybody empowers others. One of the things that does nothing to make lasting change or give people their dignity is our concept of charity. I really think if we had the right policies in the world we wouldn't need charity; everybody would be empowered and nobody would be left behind.

I know that sounds idealistic and Utopian, but deep down I believe that when we simply give people things, we are not actually inviting them to the banquet. We feel better and we can dress up in our gowns and tuxedos and go to the fundraiser, but we're still leaving people out. It's not effective.

*   *   *

I was raised by my mother who, for many years, was single and on welfare. She got some help from the community, too, but people often just dropped off the Christmas hamper and drove away. I never appreciated that. As a result, I can understand, on a micro level, the feeling of being given something and being told, "You stay over there." I don't believe in it. You have to engage people, invite them in. As a business person you say, "Come and trade with me, come and meet my friends and be a part of my network."

As a person who does volunteer work, I make similar efforts. I've had speaking engagements for kids in second-chance programs—those who were once in the justice system. A few times I've taken them, along with my kids who attend public school and my friends' kids from a local private school, down for a tour of City Hall and out to a Chinese food buffet. Why? Because I know it makes them feel engaged. They get ignited just thinking about their city and their civic engagement—and from someone, quite literally, bringing them to the banquet.

A crucial aspect of the success of these trips is anonymity. Nobody is labelled. I am the only one who knows who is who. And these kids leave with fire in their bellies—all of them.

I take the same inclusive attitude to business and to our fragrance line. I work with the government through the Canadian International Development Agency (CIDA), the federal agency leading Canada's international effort to help people living in poverty. I have met with the Ambassadors for Israel and Afghanistan and with the

Minister for Housing for the Palestinian Authority. I'm building relationships with the key people in government who are truly connecting governments to citizens in a new way.

I'm inclusive with partners as well, whether they are internal or external. For example, while we've been designing a box for the six versions of the fragrance, The Bay has asked the beauty editors from *The Globe and Mail*, as well as *More* magazine and *Flare*, to sit down with our perfumer, Brett, and me to decide which of the six scents will be our first unisex scent, to be launched on September 21, the United Nations' International Day of Peace.

All of these people—with the media involvement as a bonus—are creating this. The fact that my perfumer, Susanne Lang, is being included is a little uncommon in the world of perfume. But we all benefit from her excellent work and opinions. It's a two-way street.

But good partners are not easy to find. Part of the reason I went looking for investors/mentors on *Dragons' Den* was that no one else had stepped forward.

Nobody was willing to invest in the idea until they had proof it would work. So I did it myself. I put all the costs on my Visa card and stored the bottles in my garage when I first started. I knew the profit margin of perfume was quite high, and if I could find the right perfumer, this would be an exquisite product.

Other people tried to put up obstacles as well, including some of the journalists in Nova Scotia, where I live. When I was preparing to introduce my book, some questioned my ability to pull it off. Some were, in fact, quite cruel about it.

The product was something new, so I understood where that kind of talk came from, but it still hurt a bit.

I remember my mentor saying to me, "Come on, thick skin, broad shoulders. You're a woman out there doing this. You're going to have detractors." So I didn't pay attention to the negativity that was all around me. Looking back, I'm glad I didn't dwell on what the doubters were saying because the book is now in its third edition and ranked as a best-seller. That's why strong mentors are mandatory if you want to take risks.

Since that time, we have been more than embraced by the local media and have received so much support; the top selling Bay store in Canada is the Bay in Dartmouth, Nova Scotia—my local Bay.

I know my market and the response to my products is overwhelming. I realize I don't have to sell to everybody. It's a billion-dollar industry. I just need a slice.

And if someone tells me, "You'll never get that into the beauty counter," I always respond, "Why, is that what happened to you the last time you made a perfume?" It stops them in their tracks. It's a little cheeky, but it's Socratic! It's also very much in the vein of another quotation by philosopher Marcus Aurelius: "Why would you care about the opinion of ten thousand men if they know nothing of the subject?"

Most people are living in fear. They don't allow themselves to share their gifts when in fact it's their responsibility to do so. It's not an option. And you get past your fears very quickly when you realize it's your responsibility. So when someone comes after you from a place of fear, hit them with the Socratic Method. You hope they'll stop, but if they continue you need to remove them from your life. It's that simple.

Aurelius also said, "When you wake up, you must expect to be greeted each day with interference, ingratitude, insolence, disloyalty, ill-will and selfishness—now lead!" I feel this is critical for an entrepreneur to hear, since some people think everyone else is supposed to like what they do. That's not the way life is.

Twenty per cent of people are never going to like you. That's the reality. And if it's because you remind them of their cousin, it really has nothing to do with you. Just get on with your business. The noise this negativity makes won't be heard, and those opinions will have no bearing on what you do.

You can learn to be more skilled at shutting out distractions. It's fascinating how much the mind is like a muscle. Plato wrote about this in *The Republic*.

You take your muscles to the gym, work them hard with weights, and they rip and they strengthen because that's how they're designed. It's the same thing with our minds. We read books, we learn from wise people, and our minds are strengthened. Spiritually, if we are ignited because someone else is doing well, we strengthen our spirits.

Similarly, when we get angry or jealous or sad, we bulk up our negative side. We become bitter, lost, and jaded. It's sad—and it's limiting.

The most beautiful part is that you always have the power to begin something new. I love that. You can start in your garage with one thousand bottles of perfume.

*   *   *

Today, I don't need anybody else's money. I have more than sufficient capital with my investors and sales. The funny thing is I actually have venture capitalists calling me now. You go from begging people to help you to having everyone wanting to be on board. Now we are the source of our own capital and we generate our own momentum.

We have sourced vetiver oil from Haiti and launched our Vetiver of Haiti at The Bay with a wonderful turnout. Special guests who attended included Laureen Harper, who was there for our original launch. Minister Rona Ambrose spoke, and Minister Peter MacKay spoke and announced that I will be made an Honorary Colonel in the Canadian Military. It's a real honour to have my work recognized as part of the solution.

And I'm always working ahead on the next fragrance. We have sourced sweetie grapefruit oil of Israel for our Middle East Peace fragrance box set with discussions with suppliers. Meanwhile, we've raised our purchases of oils from Afghanistan from $2,000 to $18,000 to $60,000 USD, continuing to inject a lot of legal dollars into the economy. That injection of legal dollars into the economy of Afghanistan in a short amount of time proves it's possible, that there is the will on the part of the farmers and our supplier.

In fact, our fragrance was brought into our supplier and his contacts got some of our Noble Rose of Afghanistan to the government. As a result, the anti-narcotics officials want to do more with our supplier now that they see there is a demand from our Canadian business. If we can ignite others to come, we can get more farmers off the poppy crops.

The money goes to the right people because I personally wire it to the business owners. In the model we have, that will never be a concern. We prequalify the businesses we work with, so we know the money gets into the right hands.

People sometimes ask me what I'd do if suddenly my supply was cut off or severely delayed due to conditions in one of the countries we trade with. It doesn't concern me because, sadly, there are 33 countries facing some level of war or strife from which I can buy oils.

However, if a country can't get the oils, an opportunity is created. It lets me shine light on the story of why you can't get the perfume. If a citizen in Canada were to say, "I really want my Noble Rose perfume from Afghanistan," I'd answer, "We don't have it and we can't get any because of X, and you need to do something about it."

I'd ask them to speak to governments. Our Canadian government's policy has to change. We need to move from the model of aid to the model of trade. We need to empower businesses to be matchmakers. They should buy products from each other to bolster economies.

I'm only scratching the surface. I'm not in any way going to pretend I'm making the full difference, but the model is correct. I want others to do it too. I want a cavalry of hundreds, if not thousands, of businesses focused on trade that will cause positive change.

Brett, who met with Abdullah in Kabul when we decided to increase our investment in his company, said Adbullah was one of the top 10 business people he's ever met in his life—and he's dealt with more than a few.

Abdullah has also started schools for girls. These girls have gone on to run NGOs. They are incredible human beings in centres of influence. Of course, they have very difficult days. Some days they lose young men in their tribe to suicide bombs. It's an extremely difficult way of life.

Really, my business philosophy follows UNESCO's principle, which says: "Don't sit back and wait for government to fix the ills of society alone. We are citizens with businesses and we have the power to do more."

* * *

People sometimes ask how they can tap into their own vision and follow it. I tell them to merge what they most want to change in the world with what they most want to do. Their burning desire to see change will drive them, while their newfound career control will bring them enormous satisfaction.

Trust that if it hasn't been done before, you're probably on your way to doing something unique and significant. Don't worry, there is no book, there is no guideline; you're going to create it.

Always do your homework before you start your venture. Meet with venture capitalists and business people with experience and be sure to ask questions. I am always asking people what they think. I may incorporate some of the answers into my strategy or I may not, but I'm always asking so I can learn.

I also like to have a good time, so I incorporate that into what I do as well. For example, someone wrote me today from B.C. to let me know they had ordered one of my books and it hadn't arrived. I'm going to give them two options. They can receive two books, sent by express mail to make up for the error, or they can come and see us live on Tuesday at the Pacific Centre in Vancouver with Brett Wilson and I'll personally give them the two books.

Offering this choice makes things a bit more fun. And why not? We'll be there Tuesday and I'd love to meet them.

Besides, if you make a mistake in your business, it's got to be fixed one hundredfold. The customer must be wowed into making that 180-degree turn in their impression of your company.

I share stories about past failures in my conversations and speeches. I don't like to focus on my mistakes or on sad things that have happened, but I do demonstrate my humanity to share relevant lessons with others. I admit I am not perfect. No one should, or would, believe otherwise.

If I do something I don't think worked, which can happen any time, I go back and say, "I could have done that better. I don't want it to happen again." But I don't dwell on it or get down on myself.

I felt that way after working with my perfumer on the original order of one thousand perfume bottles. For her it was a small order. However, at the time I thought, and probably acted as if, I was the only customer. In truth she had many clients.

When we recently made the commitment to do thirty thousand bottles, I phoned her and said, "I just want to say thank you because I realize that I unduly taxed your operation when we were working on my one thousand bottles. I'm so sorry. I was new to the business and I won't do it again."

Still, I have a style, a way that's very strong and self-directed—I like everything I do to be excellent. For example, when we put out the latest edition of the book, the third edition, it probably had ten revisions. My poor designer got used to my tendency for waking up in the morning and calling with yet another change. I am pretty particular about my vision and how I want to get there, so I can be difficult to work with. I'm not negative or unkind, but I have a standard I see very clearly. But if people stay with me, it's worth it.

*   *   *

To stay positive, I only surround myself with people who are positive. The naysayers and the "you can't do it" crowd? Removed. Gossipers—they can't come over again. I'm that severe, and so in some ways I suppose I'm harsh, but I will not tolerate people tearing others down or taking pleasure in someone else's pain. There are enough dark places on this Earth and I'm not creating more. With my actions I can help make the world—and my world—more peaceful, so that's what I choose to do.

For some, a business deal that falls through or a setback in the marketplace is a catastrophe. That's because they put all their energy into the negative experience. They get completely sucked into the vortex.

On *Dragons' Den*, Kevin O'Leary called an investment in my company an emotional investment. He said there's plenty of room in the marketplace for businesses like mine but it wasn't for him. I agree. I don't think one has to make a choice between the two. I don't force others to think like me and I'm not going to become like them. I did get the chance to be the key note speaker and open for Kevin O'Leary in Halifax. I thanked him for challenging me. When he heard we landed the 91 Bay stores he said, "We have to do a follow up show about your story, this is amazing!"

It was a profit play, as well as an emotional investment. Brett will get his investment back in dividends by the year's end. When you make one thousand bottles of perfume and half of them sell in two months, even though nobody in the perfume market knows who you are, you've achieved something. Now we have on occasion outsold Chanel! We continue to steadily build our market of consumers who want values-driven products.

Our products were selling well before I went on Dragons' Den. Of course, after the show we sold out very quickly. Then it was "all hands on deck, get it out, get it out."

Another way to keep negativity out is to keep your home life separate from your work life. You may have sick kids, a relationship that's ending, or be thinking about putting your father in a home. We all deal with these types of challenges, but they can't interfere.

Clutter and all the personal troubles have no place in your work; they will end the whole dream. Keeping those separate is very stoic and very important. That is the way you get through them.

If I were to meet people and whine about my circumstances they would shut off. They would be worried if I were more focused on my own problems than theirs—and who could blame them? However, if I choose to talk about what's achievable, what's happening, and what's exciting, people will get excited.

And getting excited is easy when my book at the beauty counter might help a woman go all the way to the Senate. I think about young women going to the beauty counter—where promotion is typically dominated by movie stars or stick-thin models—and finding my book there. It thrills me to think of little girls growing up and wanting to become ambassadors or prime ministers.

Since we launched the book, I have given close to 300 talks, sometimes having done as many as three a day. It doesn't matter if I'm at a women's shelter or talking to former prisoners or to the CEOs at the Young Presidents' Organization (YPO), the philosophy and stoic wisdom is accessible to all people.

Your faith, gender, and socio-economic background are not relevant. You must work on your character, your vision, your dream, and your life, and get rid of all of the junk that stops you from really doing what you are supposed to be doing on this Earth.

The way I talk about the 7th virtue is a shift of thinking around what beauty is. The beauty in my book is the type Michelangelo made with his clay. The vision is already there; you just chisel away and let it emerge. Your beauty is your power and dignity and you are never to hand it over or strip another of it.

If young girls could realize that their beauty is their power and their dignity, maybe we'd have different kinds of behaviours, achievements, and expectations for women in government and in business.

Special, strong, intelligent, committed women are out there. I want to help nurture more of them. And in doing so, I want to change the world.

5

WHERE THERE'S A WILL, THERE'S A WAY

Turning Tragedy into Triumph

.

JIM DESLAURIER, *Director of Business Development* | **DENIS STAPLES,** *President*
Deslaurier Custom Cabinets Inc.

(*From left*) Jim Deslaurier and Denis Staples

"What we've taken away from our tragedies is the confidence to know that if we surround ourselves with people who share our vision and are willing to help us create it, we will always achieve success."

JIM DESLAURIER & DENIS STAPLES

TYPE OF BUSINESS: *Kitchen cabinet manufacturer* | FOUNDED: *Renfrew, Ontario, 1979*

www.deslaurier.ca

JIM AND DENIS TALK CANDIDLY ABOUT THEIR BUSINESS, the resilience it takes when disaster strikes, and the small community that rallied behind them.

JIM: I typically don't watch movies on TV, but on New Year's Day, 2009, my kids talked me into sitting down after supper and joining them for *The Day After Tomorrow*. If you know the movie, you know the climax is the flash freeze. A group of survivors ventured outside to find penicillin on a stranded ship and as they race back to the New York Public Library, where their only hope of survival is a fire they've kept going, the ice starts cracking all around them. My kids had the surround sound cranked up; we were at the height of the action when my son came into the room and yelled: "Dad! The shop's on fire! It's burning down!"

He had to repeat himself three times before I registered what was happening. What an eerie moment. I jumped up, got in my car, and rushed to 405 Hall Avenue in Renfrew, Ontario, where I was greeted by massive flames shooting out of the roof of our 95,000-square-foot manufacturing facility. It was 20 degrees below zero and there I was, standing helpless in sweatpants and a light shell jacket. I thought, "It's gone."

At first it seemed we might salvage some of the 150 finished kitchen orders inside, ready for delivery after Christmas. But we were told to get out and stand back as firefighters poured thousands of gallons of water on the roof, cutting holes to let the water in. It was a nightmare. In the end we were able to save about 30 kitchens, but each one had pieces that needed to be rebuilt.

Throughout the ordeal I found myself experiencing flashbacks. It wasn't the first time I'd had to stand by and watch as a fire destroyed my business. In 1986, seven years after my dad and I launched Deslaurier Custom Cabinets Inc., I had a similar adrenalin rush. It was 3:00 A.M. on a cool summer night when I was jolted awake by a cottager who called to tell me our shop was on fire. My dad's home was attached to the shop and even though the fire started in the back—where a can filled with paint rags spontaneously combusted—he could smell smoke through the attic door just outside his bedroom. He woke up, got in his wheelchair, threw a blanket over himself, and literally wheeled his chair a quarter mile to the nearest neighbour. It was traumatic. The shop was destroyed, although we were able to save and eventually rebuild his house.

What are the chances of experiencing two catastrophic fires over the life of one business? I don't really stop to dwell on it, but I guess that's part of who I am. I was taught from a very early age if there's a will, there's a way. Some people call me resilient, but I simply prefer to focus on the positive so I have the drive and energy to overcome the negative. I learned this from my father.

When I was six, my dad was working as a logger just north of Calabogie, Ontario, near Centennial Lake, when he was severely injured by a falling tree. His back was broken. He was paralyzed from the waist down and confined to a wheelchair. My dad was fairly ambitious and he didn't let this tragedy get him down. Accustomed to running his own logging business, he started a small venture out of his garage, building lawn ornaments and furniture for nearby cottagers. As the only son living at home at the time, I was his helper. By the time I reached high school I was building china cabinets when everyone else was building birdhouses. At the time, I had no intention of joining my dad's business, Jim's Pine Furniture, but as they say in the valley, I got very "handy" with woodwork.

While Dad was building small furniture and selling it from his garage I had completed high school and gone to work in construction, eventually landing a job as a forklift operator at a large food warehouse in Ottawa. When the warehouse owner got wind of my woodworking talents, he asked me to design a huge corner nook for him, and I rented space in my dad's garage to build it. My parents had recently divorced and Dad was planning to build a new home on a lot he'd purchased. Somehow he got talking to the owner of the food warehouse and between them it was decided that I would take a leave of absence to help my dad. The next thing I knew I was building a house. And, during the process, I designed my first kitchen. Then a friend of mine stopped in to see Dad's new house and liked the kitchen so much he wanted us to build one for him. While I had fully intended to return to work at the warehouse, there were so many people asking me to build cabinets that I asked my dad, "Do you want to start a business together?" He said, "Sure, son. Let's do it."

It was 1979. We literally sat in the middle of my dad's 24-by-50-foot garage, counted the lumber and the smattering of tools he had, and then I wrote him a cheque for $3,000 to solidify our partnership. Right away I planned an expansion, using a grant from the Department of Regional Economic Expansion (DREE) combined with an interest-free loan from Eastern Ontario Corp. to add 50 feet to the shop. We started out with 12 employees, growing from $150,000 in sales to about $700,000 and eventually incorporating the business in 1981. By 1986, when the first fire hit, we were up to 17 employees and hovering around the $1-million mark in sales. We had also expanded the shop to about 11,000 square feet. I was working every angle of the business, from marketing and sales to purchasing, while remaining active in finishing and installation.

That first fire was hard on my father. At 55, he was already thinking about retirement, so I opted to buy his shares. Rather than rebuild, I chose to lease the manufacturing facility on Hall Avenue in Renfrew, starting with 20,000 square feet and eventually expanding to 95,000 square feet. We had 25 employees and $2 million in annual sales, and business went on that way until 1999, when I joined forces with Ross Staples.

Ross and I met in 1994 when I was president of the Canadian Kitchen Cabinet Association (CKCA) and he was president of the Canadian Lumber Association (CLA). Coincidentally, the two of us had been running businesses out of the same building in Renfrew since 1990 but we didn't actually meet until our association work brought us together. I had Deslaurier Custom Cabinets and he was operating Madawaska Hardwood Flooring. We started to get to know each other.

In the mid-1990s, Ross sold his business and retired. I was 40 and in the process of reassessing my life. I had started out as an entrepreneur at the age of 19 and hadn't really known anything else. I was wondering what else was out there when I got into discussions with Ross.

My major frustration was that we were maintaining the status quo. We were in a rut. We weren't growing because the company wasn't generating enough cash to expand. It was not fun. In fact, I had put my confidence in one person who had practically convinced me not to grow sales in order to run a steady, stable business.

Soon Ross became my mentor. He helped me see that you have to strategically plan for growth and taught me the importance of making a plan and sticking to it. At the end of the day, he agreed to purchase an interest in Deslaurier Custom Cabinets. It couldn't have been a more perfect fit.

DENIS: When my dad, Ross Staples, sold Madawaska Hardwood Flooring, he was in his mid-sixties, but he felt he was too young to retire. He was sitting on some capital when he was approached by Jim and they were able to strike a deal. Jim wanted to take his business to the next level and he needed some assistance from a managerial standpoint—as well as an injection of cash.

Meanwhile, I had earned an Honours Degree in Commerce from McMaster University in Hamilton, Ontario, followed by an Executive Master of Business Administration from Queen's University, and was working in human resources at Madawaska Flooring. Working with my dad was probably the best experience I had. Every day we drove the hour from Ottawa to Renfrew and back again, talking about the business. He was both a counsellor and business coach.

After my dad struck the deal with Jim, I did some consulting work for Deslaurier Custom Cabinets before joining as marketing director. In November of 2005, I assumed the role of president. Right off the bat, I had an excellent relationship with Jim. He's been in the business for a long time and understands the ebbs and flows. He's been really good at grounding me and helping me understand that businesses go through cycles. You can't get too high and you can't get too low. You have to do your best to maintain an even keel.

Although Jim had retired his dad's shares in the business in 1986, his dad was still involved in the sense that he'd come by to see how things were going and to share his advice with us. So you had Jim's dad, Jim, my dad, and me. It was a couple of generations from two different families and everyone got along so well.

One of the first contributions I made to the business was to recommend we invest in an Ottawa-based showroom. Everyone was in agreement, so we went on the hunt for the right space, equipped it, staffed it, and opened it for business. That's when sales really started to take off. From 2003 to 2008 there was tremendous growth, and by December 2008, right before the second fire, we were in the best corporate shape of our history. We had record sales approaching $24 million, strong profits, and great employee morale. The entire month of January was booked over budget, which was unheard of for us. We went into Christmas feeling really great.

Then, on January 1, 2009, I got the call from our controller telling me our building was on fire. I was on the phone with Jim all night. We knew we were going to lose the plant, but we were hoping to salvage some of the finished goods inventory.

JIM: One of the great things about operating in a smaller community like Renfrew is everybody knows everybody. The assistant fire chief is a former classmate who did everything he could to help us salvage the inventory. One of the employees in our accounting department, Trudy Keller, spotted the fire from her nearby home, called it in, and was first on the scene. Luckily, Trudy had the foresight to retrieve our two main computer servers before they were damaged. We're a smart enough company to have off-site backup, but the impact of having instant access to all of our key information was immeasurable.

Half the town came out the night of the fire, including the mayor, who actually offered us temporary manufacturing space across the street so we could get back up and running quickly. Knowing that support was available, we sat down, looked over our insurance policy, determined we had sufficient coverage, and, within 10 minutes, knew we'd stay in business.

DENIS: We swiftly reassured our management team they would keep their jobs and that we weren't going to take the insurance money and run. Rather, we would reinvest and rebuild so we could come back bigger and better than ever before.

Two days after the fire, the mayor made good on her promise and we were invited to use about 50,000 square feet of empty space across the street on Hall Avenue. With 125 to 150 employees, we're considered a large employer. It was in everyone's best interest to see us stay in business. We salvaged some basic pieces of equipment and started to complete those partial orders right away.

JIM: One of our first strategies was to connect with every supplier and customer to let them know what had happened. We explained this was our tragedy but it didn't have to be theirs. Then I had to find a manufacturer who could understand the intricacies of our catalogue and produce accordingly. Eventually I found one in Sherbrooke, Quebec, whose sales were down substantially due to the downturn in the U.S. economy. Of course, the only way a deal would work was if we used our own suppliers and processes; we needed to keep the Deslaurier "machine" together without causing our suppliers to suffer. I explained we would use our own purchasing manager to source our materials, including finishes and stains, since we needed to deliver the level of quality that our customers expected.

The production management team went to Sherbrooke and basically slept in a hotel for four weeks to get them going. We produced more than 800 kitchens at their factory while rebuilding our factory. Because our showroom was still intact in Ottawa, we told our salespeople to go out and sell as per normal. We just did what we had to do, working day and night to make sure orders got filled and people were informed. In our business, everything is designed and built to order. It's our key differentiator. But it also means we need to be in control of our processes.

The loss of our facility was headline news, and every day Denis and I would be interviewed by various media outlets. Between the two of us we were hitting the papers steadily and it was always a positive story, so people continued to support and buy from us. The unwavering support we got from our builder, retail, and dealer clients allowed us to survive, a fact we won't soon forget.

We learned that when you have a situation, no matter what it is, you need to go to your customers and explain it to them in detail. You don't leave anything out. For instance, I called my builders and told them we had solid insurance coverage and we remained the best people to outsource their kitchens. I didn't just send out a letter. I did it in person or over the phone. I reassured them we would use our designers, our project coordinators, and our delivery systems. It really put them at ease.

DENIS: It's easy to be a great leader in good times, but it's not so easy in bad times. Jim taught me not to question whether we were going to get through this difficult time. Both Jim and my father had confidence in our ability to survive. They said, "It's hard. It's not fun. But we'll get through it." If you pause to feel sorry for yourself, it slows your ability to spring into action. You need to be positive and resilient. Stressing and worrying hampers your ability to focus on the action plan, which is what's going to carry you through.

While Jim was finding an outsource partner in Quebec, I called equipment suppliers, dealt with the insurance company, and started rebuilding the factory. By early summer the first pieces of new equipment had arrived. We gradually ramped up production at our new facility, eventually entering into a long-term lease with the Renfrew Industrial Commission. By the end of 2009 we were back at it, meeting all manufacturing requirements on our own.

When you go through a crisis like this you can feel sorry for yourself or you can look for the silver lining. This fire actually allowed us to automate, which meant changing our manufacturing flow and becoming more cost-competitive. We became more efficient, leaner, and more cost-effective. We also viewed this as an opportunity to change from solvent-based to water-based finishes and become a greener facility. Finally, we revamped our catalogue, doubling our standard offerings and introducing a new modern cabinetry line.

JIM: Out of this disaster came an opportunity and now I can't see how we could have created anything better than what we have. Suddenly we had a state-of-the-art operation capable of supporting our growth while meeting a lot of the environmental expectations for the future. It was an amazing accomplishment.

It's important to mention that Denis was very diligent about our insurance coverage. He had constantly followed up on the recommendations made by our insurance agent. For example, he arranged for regular inspections of our shop and had a complete inventory of our equipment conducted, including pictures and appraised values. This was instrumental in helping us settle with the insurance company and start the rebuilding process.

DENIS: I learned you need to review your insurance policy every year to make sure you have the appropriate coverage. The one thing that saved us is that I was involved personally in the review of our insurance. I credit the foresight of our agent at Lumbermen's Underwriting Alliance. He insisted on meeting with me, since I was Deslaurier's president, to go over our policy. Starting a couple of years prior to the fire, I met with him annually. He was the one who recommended we upgrade from six to 12 months of business interruption insurance coverage, which, as you can appreciate, was critical to our survival.

I only wish I had done a better job at preparing for a potential disaster beyond insurance by having an emergency preparedness plan in place. It would have helped to answer the question, "What will we do if tomorrow we lose everything?" During a tragedy there's a tremendous amount of pressure; you're stressed, you're tired, and it's obviously a dangerous time to be making important decisions. Yet many of these decisions must be made with lightning speed. To have considered these things when we were calm would have been very helpful.

JIM: My father always said, "Each day is a new one, and you never know what situation you may face tomorrow." He saw the importance of planning for the future, which includes protecting your future and making sure your insurance is adequate and up-to-date at all times.

In business, my dad and I, as well as Denis and Ross Staples, have always agreed that we must stick to our core values and, most importantly, be fair and honest, giving people around us the opportunity to do the same.

If you give people the opportunity to be fair, you can create win–win situations. It's like telling your kids what time they need to be home on a Friday night. You can't just tell them to be in by 10 P.M. You have to understand their reasons for perhaps not agreeing and be willing to negotiate something fair. In business, if you're fair with everybody, they catch on quickly and they either try to be fair in return—which is the right thing to do—or they don't. And if they don't, you need to say, "See you later."

DENIS: It's a bit ironic because my dad always told me that Lumbermen's Underwriting Alliance had a reputation for being fair. It's the main reason we've stayed with them through the years. And that's exactly how they operated after the fire. They were fair, they were reasonable, and it really helped us in the rebuilding process. It allowed us to focus on our real motivation: looking out for our customers and our employees.

There are 125 people who rely on us to be able to make mortgage payments and car payments, pay rent, and buy food, insurance, trips, and all the rest. That was probably the one aspect arising from the fire that was most difficult for us. We went from everyone complaining January was overbooked to not knowing if they would have a job at all. Thanks to our insurance coverage there was a whole group of people who could breathe a sigh of relief, knowing they would be paid whether they worked or not. We know all our employees personally, and this is a responsibility we take very seriously. We may be in the business of building cabinets, but we're also building people.

JIM: In order to reach our company and personal goals, we simply won't take no for an answer. Sometimes we have to take a second, third, even a fourth or fifth try, but if we believe we can make something happen—and the expectation is realistic—we will make it happen. This motto has proven itself accurate time and time again. Sure, we've experienced tremendous challenges, but we've turned those challenges into great opportunities.

What we've taken away from our tragedies is the confidence to know that if we surround ourselves with people who share our vision and are willing to help us create it, we will always achieve success. It might be a good lesson for other entrepreneurs to note. It has certainly worked for us.

6

A CHAIN AND A NEIGHBOUR

You Can Be Both

STEPHEN McINTOSH

Factory Optical / Optiks International / EyecandyOptiks

"There is no such thing as too much competition
if you do what you do very well."

STEPHEN McINTOSH

TYPE OF BUSINESS: *Retail optical chain, manufacturer* | FOUNDED: *Regina, Saskatchewan, 1999*

www.factoryoptical.ca

MY COMPANY WAS FORMED IN THE SUMMER OF 1999, when I decided to buy a single retail optical outlet with an antiquated one-person lens fabrication lab. The purchase was, in retrospect, mostly born of necessity.

I had left a promising corporate banking career a few years earlier to assume a general manager's position with a growing chain of retail optical stores. The company had been a banking client of mine. In this position I was subservient to the founder/owner but positioned above his only son. The space between the two began to get tight, you might say, and my future there did not contain much upside.

Originally, the plan was for me to move to the west and open more stores, but the owner and I differed on execution. I decided instead to buy his sole Western Canadian operation.

There were eight stores in southwestern Ontario, where I lived with my wife and children, and one in Regina, Saskatchewan. Back then, they were called Wholesale Vision stores in Ontario, while the one in Regina was called Factory Optical.

It was a major life decision. I was moving my wife and two small boys from London, Ontario, to Regina, a city they had never even visited. We knew absolutely no one there. This was quite an overwhelming time for a young family.

My business started out with considerable opportunity for failure. We began with a $30,000 debit balance in our current account, and we owed our legal counsel $20,000 for doing the acquisition. We also owed the vendor another $30,000 for the working capital left in the company.

I recognized immediately that I had overpaid for the business. I had a very short period of time to solicit financing for the purchase and, consequently, little time for due diligence. At the time I didn't see this as a problem since I had been familiar with the operation as the store's GM, albeit, geographically, at arm's-length.

But we were very lucky in a number of ways, all of which collectively not only paved the road for us to get where we are today, but in the absence of which we would no doubt have failed quickly and dramatically.

During the purchase I was trying to establish banking facilities in Regina by telephone from London. After securing the private equity funding necessary to fund the purchase of the company, we needed an operating facility to finance working capital. I was referred to a very young and inexperienced banker in Regina who pleaded our case to his adjudication group, but the result was an authorization of only half the monies I required, subject to the personal guarantees of my 17 equity investors.

This was a true dealbreaker; it would have fundamentally undermined the spirit of equity investing. After all, I had gone out and pleaded, begged, and borrowed from friends and family, and it had taken 17 people to reach the $560,000 purchase price for the company, in consideration of which I provided them a 49 per cent collective interest.

As an alternative, this young banker allowed me to rewrite the credit application myself, and we were provided double the original funding requested with no personal guarantees to speak of. We were now capitalized to go forward.

The market appeal of my Ontario initial public offering of August 1999 was grounded in the fact that I issued each of the 17 investors two classes of shares—common shares, reflective of their individual ownership position, and preferred shares, reflective of their actual dollar investment. The preferred shares had to be fully redeemed prior to the declaration of any dividends on the common shares.

In other words, everyone got their full investment back before dividends were eligible on the remaining common shares in perpetuity. The investors would have their money out before I personally would see a nickel beyond salary. In my opinion, it was a responsibly structured and fair agreement.

But, as I said, I know I overpaid. By how much? Who knows? On a $560,000 purchase, did I pay $50,000 too much? That Factory Optical store in Regina was technically my baby, along with the Ontario stores. I don't blame anyone for it.

I had made a couple of trips out there, done my thing, but what ended up happening—and this is the reality of this kind of transaction—is that when I agreed to buy that store in Regina, I was still working in London and the clock was ticking. I had an August 17 drop-dead date for raising the money.

That was a stressful time during which I was selling air. Nobody among my friends and family—and my investors—knew anything about the optical business or anything about Regina. They couldn't touch this company that they were investing in. That was tough, because it was both stressful and time-consuming. On August 18, I would likely be out of work if the deal fell through.

I knew even during the process there were things I wasn't catching, but I had enough faith in my ability to make this work that I thought, "Even if I have to take a little step backwards that I didn't anticipate, this is a marathon, not a sprint, and down the road I'll still end up winning."

Then reality hit. The first two nights I was in Regina, I went through six months of historical retail customer transactions and found our incidence of up-selling on core product at the store to be almost non-existent. Our ophthalmic frame inventory was stale and heavily replicated. The lens manufacturing equipment was easily three generations old, and the physical premises were in considerable need of repair. Also, in the acquisition I had assumed the management of four retail staff and one dedicated lab person, most of whom were substandard.

However, early on I did profit from some quick victories. In an unprecedented coup, I managed to talk the two largest ophthalmic frame suppliers in North America into buying back stale inventory at the price I had paid for it. I still take my hat off to them today for that gesture and for their ongoing loyalty.

We now had marketable product to sell, and we had been given supplier pricing and terms that should not have been afforded an operation of our size. This had the most profound effect in the early days, as our pricing gave us a competitive advantage relative to much larger competitors.

This advantage continues to this day and, I believe, is the result of our having been able to consistently execute on plan, not disappointing those who extended themselves to assist us during our early growth spurt.

The other early win for us, and perhaps the most significant, occurred in October 1999 when I rolled the dice on the marketing side.

As I explained, when I got there we were not strong financially. The store I bought was founded in 1983 and, 16 years later, nothing had changed. You could lay a ruler across the stagnant sales line. So it was a crapshoot. Honestly, I tell people today, "If October 1999 hadn't worked, we wouldn't be having this conversation."

Over the 36 months before I bought it, the store had seen sales of about $42,000 per month, and this didn't change during the first full month I owned it: September 1999. The next month I injected $15,000 of my own funds into advertising, and we undertook an ambitious radio campaign for the 31 days of October.

The result was an incredible $120,000 sales month for October 1999—almost a threefold growth. Profits were poured into a comparable campaign for November and December, and this practice continued for many months thereafter.

Up to then, radio had not been a prevalent media vehicle for our market category. Today, we are the largest radio advertiser in every single market in which we operate, and I believe this has been a very real catalyst for our success.

Still, the risk of this whole exercise was compounded by the fact that, contrary to the radio stations' collective advice, I elected to write and voice my own spots. These spots often had little to do with retail optical and were often opinion pieces of mine. I relied heavily on 60-second spots rather than the traditional 30-second price/sale-oriented spots. This is a practice we continue to use.

As I said, we funnelled money back into our marketing efforts, and we did that before any of our competitors could figure out what we were doing. By the time they did, it was too late to catch up. Today we do this in every market because we can afford to, but when we were doing it then, I'd say we were just being bold. And it worked because, suddenly, we were the market share leader.

* * *

Of course, getting to that leadership position is not all about intuition and lightning-quick strategic moves. One of the keys to achieving success is being able to visualize it ahead of time.

In my 1999 business plan, I established quantifiable targets that remain in effect today. (Any shortcomings around targets by this point I attribute to the fact that we have broadened our operations to areas that had not been originally contemplated.) To be specific, I had pledged to develop a network/retail distribution reach of 30 stores in Western Canada in 15 years. A dozen years later, we sit at 17, and we anticipate adding five additional stores in the next 18 to 24 months.

I had established a gross revenue target of $30 million annually in 15 years. We will gross $20 million this year and $30 million is attainable over the next 18 to 24 months. The single store we originally purchased did a little over $500,000 in gross revenues annually.

The stores we build now are not modelled on anything that came before. The typical footprint of an optical store in Canada is probably 1,400 square feet, while our last four have ranged from 8,000 to 12,000 square feet, with on-site manufacturing, optometry, and designer sunglass boutiques.

But don't let anyone tell you we are simply a chain of optical stores. Let me tell you why.

I tour our stores every few months, because we are always opening new ones and hiring new people. I take everyone out for dinner and drinks, and pitch my program to new staff. Recently, in one exercise, I had everybody grab a napkin or a piece of paper and write down our elevator speech. I asked them: "If you had 15 seconds to tell someone in an elevator who we are, what would you say?"

I got good answers, bad answers, and everything in between. The right answer is this: we are a chain of neighbourhood stores.

If you really analyze that phrase, you'll see that it's an oxymoron. But the chain part is the critical mass that we've been fortunate enough to attain, which allows us to bring product to market as cost-effectively as possible. It also allows us to capitalize on economies of scale and certain synergies—all that good stuff they taught me in MBA school.

The neighbourhood store description is our significant differentiator. In my experience, you get a different feeling when you walk into a boutique with an owner/operator, as compared to a big chain or a big-box store. I want to replicate that owner/operator boutique feeling in the stores. We've taken big strides to accomplish this.

But we don't have a policies and procedures manual. Never have, never will. We hire smart people and we empower them. Our policies and procedures can be contained on the back of a matchbox. Put two sentences on there and you've got it covered. For our people working in a Factory Optical store it's this: imagine every day that you own it, and imagine every single second that you're there what it's like to be on the other side of the table—pretend you're a customer.

If you are constantly doing these two things you're going to make the right decision 80 per cent of the time—and, because you're trying, clients won't get mad at you the other 20 per cent of the time.

We recognized a long time ago that there aren't a lot of people buying prescription eyewear because they love it. They're buying it because they have to. So we do the little things others may not.

Some of these higher-end optical stores take it upon themselves to stack a bunch of frames in a pile on a desk because it looks neat. If I were a customer, this would drive me absolutely nuts. I want to see the price. I want to distinguish the frames from each other. I want them laid out for me.

At our stores, everything has a price and a program, and we're not trying to get you out of there quickly because we don't like you, we're trying to get you out of there quickly because we know you don't like it.

We don't locate our stores in malls; we locate them in strip malls or in power centres because I think it's important that you can drive up to the front door, walk in, have someone greet you by name, make a purchase, and get out.

Really, we're much more like a mattress store than, say, a pharmacy. You buy a mattress every eight years. You might go into the pharmacy every month. We don't have the luxury of that kind of constant contact. People actually buy glasses about every three years, depending on their coverage, so we've got to kill them with kindness whenever we get the chance.

We really try to remember everybody's name and do all these sorts of little—but extremely important—things. We don't move staff around, even when we have multiple stores in a single market, because it undermines their ability to create continuity in their customer relationships.

Many of these little things are very subtle, I think. The chain part is self-explanatory. The neighbourhood store part is what we strive for every day. These are the day-to-day challenges, and we all work together at solving them.

But sometimes I'm dealing with issues on my own. What keeps me up at night is any failure relative to my expectations. My expectations are very high. I've got really good people, and I push them and work them really hard.

I'll give you an example of the type of struggle I face. We're doing some serious safety eyewear business in the oil sands now, as sort of an offshoot of a company that we set up. I'm doing everything I can to over-service—that's such a cliché in the business world—but in fact I'm really, genuinely passionate about it. It's not so much a revenue-driven effort, it's that I've gotten to know the people at the other side of it and I don't want to disappoint them.

I'm the same way with my employees—and with my customers in the field. On our website, there's a link allowing people to write in to the president. Rarely does a day go by that I'm not talking to a customer or prospective customer of ours via that medium. If I get information from them that I find unsettling, it can keep me up all night.

I realize that in these cases I'm only hearing from one single person and that presidents with operations of a similar magnitude think I'm moronic to dwell on these problems the way I do. Still, I'll often spend the first half hour of a day answering back and forth with a customer, having a dialogue with them, and trying to apologize and/or explain how we do things. In my humble opinion, this is the single greatest source of company and industry feedback available to me. I feel like I return to university every single day.

For example, I got an e-mail recently from a fellow who thought our radio ad was a bit misleading. We used this 2-for-1 merchandising platform, which is proprietary and unlike anything in our business, the biggest in the country. But not every single frame is included, due to licensing restrictions with the frame vendors. He wanted the second "free" frame for his child under our 2-for-1 offer, but it was a frame that fell under the restrictions. He said, "I'm just a little concerned, and I think I've been misled." I obsessed about that all night. That's the kind of thing that will probably kill me early, but I have to do it.

I'd argue that the fact I care so much is an advantage rather than a disadvantage. I think it makes for a long day for me. That half hour in the morning is a half hour I could be doing something else. But caring is a huge advantage. If I didn't care, how could I ensure we keep improving? I'm happy when my customers are happy.

My father used to say, "If you get up in the morning and are excited about going to work, and then at the end of the day you are excited about going home, then you have it all figured out." That motivates me.

I am very lucky because a lot of the thankless "heavy lifting" at our company has been done and now we're on to the fun stuff—the growth, the opportunity to be creative about how we do things, and the chance to mentor and help govern the evolution and maturity of key young people in our organization. I am motivated by the fact that I have fun at work and have fun when I'm not at work. I cannot even envision retirement.

This kind of success obviously requires perseverance. For example, I've never uttered the phrase "That'll never work," and if someone says something like that to me, I always say, "Convince me why." I don't pretend to have the right answer to anything, but I will presume it to be right until confronted with enough compelling testimony to the contrary.

Every decision should be weighed against the possible downside. If the downside is not too deep and not too harmful, then the best way to answer that question is to test it yourself. You are bound to learn things in the process.

For example, we have surprising seasonality in the optical retail business. November and December are horrible months. People are not spending money on themselves at Christmas, and prescription eyewear is not exactly an attractive gift option. For three consecutive years, I heavily promoted Christmas gift cards on the radio that were worth $120 but on sale for $100. This failed to work each time. Now I know definitively that Christmas is our time to "clean up and don't worry about sales."

On the other hand, it might be too dangerous to simply test one of your theories. When I started my business and rolled the dice on an expensive advertising campaign in my second month of ownership, I put into practice some basic lessons I learned about marketing.

Tough economic times will come to every business eventually, including small businesses. The sad reality is that advertising is one of those expenses that any business owner would deem to be discretionary—certainly more so than his or her own salary.

The Catch-22 of the whole thing is that, when belts get tightened, a lot of businesses quickly pull their advertising. Well, that's your lifeline. That's absolutely the one thing you should try to preserve at all costs, even if it means eating less yourself. I see it happen all the time. It's just a knee-jerk reaction, and once you undo it, you can't redo it. So that's when not to pull the plug on advertising.

Alternatively, when to pull the trigger on advertising is, in my humble opinion, anytime. Any ad house will tell you the same thing. It's a frequency game. The guy who opens his store and buys an ad every Saturday on the radio is burning dollar bills on his front lawn.

You have to commit to a program and stick with it. That's job one. Job two is to differentiate yourself on the radio. You flip the dial today and every station is just droning white noise. Right or wrong—and it turned out to be right, I think—I made a conscious decision back in 1999 that I was not going to let the hyped-up radio guy do my spots for me; I was going to do them myself.

I think this lends a little bit of credibility and genuineness to the whole thing. But I don't even necessarily talk about my business in each spot. It sounds arrogant and I don't mean it that way, but we've generated a bit of a following because people want to hear what I have to say.

In fact, in the spots, I'll talk about experiences I've had in other stores and mention how great they were. I'll talk philosophically about what I think businesses need to be doing. It's not necessarily altruistic. If I'm criticized for anything, it's for being too high-brow sometimes because I'm a bit of an academic myself, and I sometimes speak in business language that isn't always understood. People who do get it, love it. I'll do a 60-second spot on my relationship with my employees and it'll have nothing to do with selling eyewear. But it seems to work.

Of course, I don't pretend to be perfect.

We elevated our game somewhat two years ago when we set up a second holding company and brought in a very progressive venture capital firm as a minority shareholder in that company. With that came considerable growth capital.

But we probably could have expedited our evolution considerably if we had done this earlier. One could argue that corporately we weren't ready earlier on, but cerebrally we certainly were.

Also, I likely could have benefitted by surrounding myself with some sort of advisory group or committee. I have three university degrees, a solid business background, I think, and a position of ownership in a tiny retail environment. I am surrounded by many great optical people, but not necessarily people possessing a level of business acumen from which I have benefitted. That might have been an advantage.

But you learn a lot by taking the road I have taken.

One thing I would tell any budding entrepreneur is that you must persevere—especially when negotiating. Sounds simple, but you would be surprised how many don't embrace this reality. Without sounding too flippant, a wise man once gave me two pieces of advice:

1. "As long as you are writing the cheque, you have the hammer." I remind myself of this every day and it has provided me the fortitude to ask for more than I deserve and only occasionally settle for what I do deserve; and,

2. "Enter every negotiation knowing more about what the other guy does for a living than he knows about what you do." I do research before I meet people. This does not necessarily entail formal research as much as often just permitting myself the time to really contemplate their business world and how we might fit into it.

In my humble opinion, there is no such thing as too much competition if you do what you do very well. And, if you have a good reputation, it's always easier to move to new areas of the market.

All those years ago, when I bought that single store in Regina, I bought the name Factory Optical. Today, the way we're structured is a little bit complicated, but all our stores in Saskatchewan now trade as Factory Optical. And we've opened lots of stores in Alberta and B.C. since then. They all trade as Optiks International.

But now we're in the process of rolling out a third brand in Saskatchewan. It's a chain of sunglass boutiques, or designer sunglass stores. They're called EyecandyOptiks. So far, we've got three of those set up. We just started in 2010.

We deal with all of the designer frame companies on the optical side, and because of the volume we do, we get good pricing from practically everyone. The wholesale discounts that we receive on eye frames typically apply to the corresponding designer sunglasses in the same collection. For example, our pricing on Dolce & Gabbana optical product is the same for our Dolce & Gabbana sunglasses. That's a real competitive advantage. We compete with other sunglass companies that don't have that luxury.

As well, we have cross-promotional opportunities. For example, we always position our sunglass boutiques right next to one of our optical stores. If you buy contact lenses at our optical store, you can get a deal on your sunglasses next door. Or, if you buy sunglasses at the EyecandyOptiks store and you want to put prescription lenses in them, you can go next door and have it done at a better price.

If you shop in our big stores—the 10,000-square-foot ones that we've opened in the last few years—you can visit a sunglass boutique right inside that store.

Why are we still here today? Above all else, I believe that I was highly motivated to own my own business—as many are—and I had both the confidence to try and the full support of my wife. Many don't have those elements in place when they start out, and I have seen an inordinate number of similarly sized businesses fail.

One concession I did provide my wife at that time was that I would spend less time at the office and more time at home. I had been a corporate banker and had worked long hours in the past. In the end I believe I managed to keep my promise. I never missed a kid's hockey, football, or lacrosse game, never missed a school function, and I was able to work in the early years from home.

Finally, don't be afraid to include others in the process, but be sure to reward them in the aftermath. Of course, my wife has been instrumental in my professional journey. I have key personnel who have capabilities I don't and upon whom I rely heavily. Then there are my beloved investors.

That single original retail store I bought in Regina 11 years ago is still there. The antiquated one-person lens fabrication lab has been replaced by two wholly owned state-of-the art conventional and digital labs. The original manufacturing space has been converted to an optometric practice. Revenues out of that original location have, by today, doubled.

We've had great success, yes, but I think my biggest thrill probably hasn't happened yet.

I love the fact that I, along with others, have created something tangible, something that I can touch. I am truly excited by the prospect, whether realizable or not, that we are building something sustainable and of such a critical mass that perhaps my sons can one day assume the leadership.

7
TECHNOLOGY LEADERSHIP AND
THE ART OF TAKING CONTROL

GAYLE ROBIN

President and Co-founder, StrategicAmpersand

"Keep a lens focused on the bottom line …
You must have a financial infrastructure in place."

GAYLE ROBIN

TYPE OF BUSINESS: *Technology-focused marketing and communications* | FOUNDED: *Toronto, Ontario, 1991*

www.stratamp.com

TRUTHFULLY, MY ENTREPRENEURIAL JOURNEY might have ended prematurely in 1990 when I decided to sell the agency I'd started, Ampersand Marketing. We specialized in direct marketing, corporate communications, and public and media relations. At the time I was already outsourcing work in certain non-core areas, and I really wasn't enjoying the stress of running an agency on my own. I was quite miserable having all the pressure resting solely on me.

So I decided to sell the business. I took out a blind ad in a trade magazine and received about a dozen replies. My husband, Michael, a CA who specialized in mergers and acquisitions, did the groundwork for me.

We went through the search process for about a year, and he identified several potential buyers. He met with the four companies we thought looked most promising. One of the companies told me that my company was worthless and that my accounts were lousy, but they'd hire me to work for them as a vice-president. Another said there was no market for an agency that did only business-to-business work, and that beer, cars, and tobacco were the only true cash cows. The third was an industrial agency with four male partners, all close to 60, in brown and orange offices near the airport. Not promising.

The last was a small agency run by two partners—but they didn't want to buy, they wanted to merge. We met with them three or four times. They seemed nice enough, their work looked good, and they were the right size—about the same size as us. But something was bugging me. I finally asked my husband if they were married. He asked me if it would make a difference, and I told him: "If they're married, I'm not interested." They were, but Michael told me to sit tight and not count them out completely—that it would all depend on how we structured the shareholders' agreement.

We spent six months negotiating our deal—one in which I couldn't be outvoted. When it was signed, I moved into their offices. The next few years were spent building, building, and building. After the fifth year, three partners became two. We had found a niche in the technology industry and became respected for our expertise. We were moving in the right direction.

Fast-forward 20 years. Today we are a multimillion-dollar integrated communications agency specializing in the technology industry, ranking somewhere in the top 50 in Canada in terms of revenue. We have a solid balance sheet and I believe a good reputation. Our clients are the who's who of the technology industry and more than half our client base has been with us for a decade or more.

Of course, that's not the whole story. Before I decided to become someone's business partner, I became a business person myself—and trust me, I started early.

*   *   *

I grew up in a single-parent household in the 1960s in Ottawa. My mother worked as a secretary, but making ends meet was tough. There was little in the way of daycare, babysitters were expensive, and school lunch programs didn't exist. I learned at a very early age to be self-sufficient. I had to entertain myself, and more was expected of me than the average kid. Being independent became second nature.

In the late 1960s my mother was diagnosed with manic depression—today you'd say she has bipolar disorder. For several years her life was psychiatric wards, medications, shock treatments, and long absences. My grandparents helped financially but couldn't visit often since, by then, we had moved to Toronto and they were still in Ottawa—four-and-a-half hours away by car. Meanwhile, mental illness was misunderstood, shameful, and never discussed, certainly not with a child. It wasn't easy on either of us.

When my mother eventually got back on her feet and was able to function—with the help of a new wonder drug called lithium—my grandfather decided to get her busy running her own company. He was in the jewellery business and at one time owned 20 stores. He decided my mother should become a jewellery importer and wholesaler.

My mother travelled to Italy and imported gold jewellery, which she sold to retailers all across the province of Ontario, from Windsor to the Quebec border, driving upwards of 200,000 kilometres a year. She could handle buying, selling, and filling orders, but bookkeeping was beyond her. So at the age of 11, I was taught how to do it all—invoices, monthly statements, tagging inventory, issuing supplier cheques, and making all the accounts payable and receivable ledger entries. In short, I was a controller before I was a teenager.

Unless you knew me you couldn't possibly imagine the irony of this job title. As a kid who had been helpless to control her own challenging environment, I soon learned that I had to find a way to control things if I were to have any hope of feeling secure.

I worked my way through high school and university, always with a part-time job. After school I went into sales—first in personnel, then in the health and beauty business, where at the age of 22 I was promoted to a position I was totally unqualified for—national sales manager for what was then the largest health and beauty aid distributor in Canada. I had 25 sales reps, most of whom were between 35 and 55 and male, and we sold over a thousand different products. I had complete responsibility for all forecasting, pricing, promotions, and head office sales. And I didn't have a clue. I was definitely not in control.

But I learned by asking, listening, thinking, and by making mistakes. My grandfather reminded me that I worked for my staff, they didn't work for me. I was there only to make them successful, and I couldn't make them successful by trying to control them.

As you can imagine, considering my control issues, working for other people was difficult. Eventually I became disillusioned.

This was especially true during my next job, as regional sales and key account manager at an international cosmetics company. In my first year I exceeded my revenue targets by 100 per cent. My compensation was a combination of a base salary plus a defined bonus based on reaching a stated revenue target. When it came time to pay out the bonus, my boss told me the company never thought I'd actually make the numbers, and that they had never paid anyone such a high bonus. Overall, they had not done well that year and, besides, the president felt that it was a fluke. Then he handed me a cheque for one-tenth the amount owed to me with an insincere apology. In a fit of melodrama, I ripped up the cheque and told them if the company was in such trouble they needed the money more than I did.

Yes, I stayed on with the company. Outraged, but determined to prove my managers wrong, I swallowed hard and did it again. But this time I exceeded my quota by 300 per cent, marched into the president's office and demanded the money I was owed, along with a promotion. He was 64 years and 11 months old—one month away from retirement from the company where he had worked for 30 years. His response was: "Take a look around and tell me if you see any other women in management at this company." He also told me that I was too good on the road to be promoted and that I should know my place. My jaw dropped. I asked him if he wasn't afraid I would take legal action for discrimination and breach of contract. He smiled and calmly told me he was one month away from retirement. "Sweetheart," he said smugly, "do whatever the hell you want because I won't be around to deal with it." Needless to say, I quit.

While moping around and deciding I didn't want to be in sales anymore, where I couldn't control other aspects of the business such as delivery, quality, manufacturing, or inventory, I heard about a company that needed some sales and marketing advice. So I helped that client. Then I helped another, and another. It seemed I was now a consultant.

For me, that meant having meetings and writing reports and getting paid to do both. But I quickly figured out that presenting reports that ended up in a drawer wasn't gratifying. The companies usually agreed with the recommendations, but they wanted someone to actually implement the strategies; they wanted someone to control the processes.

Control was a concept I understood. Though my marketing skills were good and my selling skills great, I didn't actually know how to execute the tactics. I had always relied on those who did that for a living: the advertising/marketing agencies.

So slowly I started to hire people to do the things I didn't know how to do, such as designing ads and direct mail pieces and carrying out public relations activities. I wrote all the proposals, most of the copy, learned about how ink got onto paper, managed all of the production, did all of the operations stuff, like the bookkeeping. And, of course, I did the selling.

I learned from everyone I hired, as well as the freelancers and, most especially, my suppliers. I remembered my grandfather's lesson—listen and learn from those who know. I went to every seminar and trade show that could help me. I read stacks of books on marketing, management, direct mail, advertising, public relations, employee relations, and building companies. I revelled in the lessons I could glean from Jack Welch, Leo Burnett, Lester Wunderman, and Lee Iacocca, to name a few.

I knew knowledge meant success, so I made sure I was constantly plugged in. I knew my business's bank balance every day, the profit or loss of every project, as well as what we were good at and what we weren't. I knew who had paid us and who hadn't. I also knew we needed an operating facility from a bank.

I still remember going to my first bank meeting and how relieved I was to find out the bank manager was a woman, since I was sure she would be empathetic. I was prepared. I had arrived with a business plan, which included my first year's financial statement as well as my current accounts payable and accounts receivable schedules. I was ready to wow her.

There were a few niceties—but these soon ended as I realized she just didn't understand what we did as a company because she couldn't touch, feel, or count it. She hadn't heard of any of our clients, who were mostly small companies and one big U.S. business-to-business technology company that consumers hadn't heard of.

She wanted to know if I had assets, collateral, or a mortgage-free house. Then she asked if I had any cash. Because, you see, if I had cash then the bank would loan me their cash, but I'd have to give them mine as security. After a few futile minutes passed she asked the dreaded question: "Couldn't your husband or father co-sign for you?" I don't remember what I said, but it could not have been pleasant. I left angry, but knowing if I came back and showed them hard evidence—a string of positive results—next time they'd listen.

After my third year in business, my sales were over $1 million and we had been profitable all three years. I knew the banks would talk to me, but this time I would be selective and find someone I could relate to—someone who could understand my business. I shopped around for the right bank manager and I didn't ask for very much money, just enough to cover the gap between when we billed and when we got paid. I took out small, short-term loans and paid them back early. I met with my banker every three months, but I took him out for lunch to tell him what we were up to and how we were doing.

But, despite all these good things, I was stressed, tired, and scared. The whole business rested on everything I controlled—sales, staff, payroll, collecting money, and various other tasks.

This is why, as I explained, I ultimately merged my business with Miles Pollock's business, Strategic Marketing. My husband had originally suggested I get a partner, but I didn't want a partner. Not because I couldn't share the business, but because I knew I would have to give up some of the control. Somehow I decided to take a risk and give it a try.

* * *

My agency, Ampersand Marketing, which I started in 1985, was at the time a business-to-business agency specializing in direct marketing, corporate communications, and public and media relations. Miles had started his agency, Strategic Marketing, in 1981. It was a sales promotion and advertising agency specializing in the retail sector.

When we initially got together, we had a really strange mix of clients. My largest client was Oracle, and Strategic Marketing's largest client was Woolco, which ended up being bought by Walmart. After about a year together I suggested we make a bold move and focus on the technology side of the business, since it was the early days of the industry and the streets seemed to be paved with gold. It was also very incestuous; it didn't matter which clients you worked with and nobody cared about conflicts. When we worked with Oracle, we worked with all the hardware vendors and nobody seemed to care. The technology sector specialization also offered us a good opportunity to differentiate ourselves.

Though we had made the decision to specialize in technology, everything happened in an interesting way. It was a very organic thing.

Since the technology industry was in its infancy, it often appeared to our clients that what we did was rocket science. This was partly because the industry wasn't doing much marketing in those days, especially direct marketing. And almost no one was using public relations. Some were making use of advertising, but really not much else. Companies saw magic in what we did because the people running these businesses were not marketers; they were either engineers or former salespeople.

Our goal was to become the best integrated marketing communications agency that offered a full complement of services to the technology industry.

In those days the concept of integrated marketing/communications was burgeoning and while we were a truly integrated agency, many others weren't. In the first five years as StrategicAmpersand, we saw a lot of consolidation in the industry as the big players bought up a lot of the smaller niche, specialty agencies. Huge agencies would say: "Oh, we believe in integrated marketing/communications," but then they would just add a PR division and a direct response division and continue to run them separately. This meant clients never ever derived the benefits of an integrated strategy.

The siloed or divisionalized model is incredibly frustrating. Clients have to deal with five or six different agency contacts, which is slow and inefficient. On top of this, they have to hope all these contacts communicate with each other so their messaging and positioning are the same, and that doesn't happen very often. And, if it does happen, it is an extremely expensive exercise for the client.

Big agencies really had no concept of the power of integrating all of these MarCom services, nor did they have the ability to run their businesses that way. They couldn't, because they were too big.

So, in the early days, we had a huge advantage. Our clients had access to a full complement of integrated MarCom services without having to deal with multiple people in multiple divisions of one big agency or with multiple agencies, all of whom were fighting over their dollars because they had separate P&Ls.

When I used to get asked who our competition was, I'd answer: "We don't have any," and I really believed that. Sure, PR agencies came along that specialized in technology, but there were really no other truly integrated agencies that did. There might have been a direct response agency or an ad agency that had a technology client or two, but nobody other than us did everything.

Things took off relatively quickly for StrategicAmpersand. Once we became established, it was a very short time before we became known as "the tech agency" in the city. The biggest challenge, honestly, in the first five years, was keeping up. Just keeping up was unbelievable.

I attribute much of our success at that time to ignorance and fear, which kept us moving. I didn't know what I didn't know, so I wasn't really afraid to hit the ground running.

Luckily, seeing that I was a complete control freak, my partner Miles let me run with the job of setting up our evolving infrastructure and deciding on the agency's new direction. When I had said, "You know, I think we should be a tech agency," he sort of shrugged and said, "Sure, okay." The fact that our styles were so completely different—that I was such an obsessive driver and he was so much more laid back—helped a lot.

For me, fear has always been a driving factor. Being a perfectionist, I had a fear of failure and felt compelled to push harder every day. I didn't ever want to lose business to anyone else.

Sure there were rough times. In 2001 the tech bubble burst and the market collapsed and we faced serious challenges. But, because we had been focused and principled during the dot-com boom, we stayed alive when others didn't.

Our policy was that we never took paper; we never, ever took shares in our clients. Even in those days when companies were beating down the doors to get to us, my answer always was, "Paper doesn't help me make my payroll." We never took on start-ups—or at least we didn't take on "the two guys with a great idea working out of their house." Clients had to be funded and they had to have cash.

Our strategy was always to have clients with first-, second-, or third-place market share, but during the lean times the big guys stopped spending. From 2001 to about 2004, we were steadfast about sticking with technology and consumer electronics companies.

In tough times you take business where you can get it. When our clients' executives moved out of the technology industry and they called us, we didn't turn them away. We retained certain criteria around the type of clients we'd work with and went after, and those years were extremely difficult. It really wasn't until 2007 or 2008 that we really started to see a shift back to a healthier technology industry.

The result is we have broadened our client base slightly. Now we include financial services clients. It's not such a leap. These clients are often focused on providing technology-based solutions for their clients. There is a tangential tie.

Those executives who engage us when they join new companies are demonstrating their loyalty and trust in our abilities. This is why, as I said before, more than half our client base has been with us for a decade or more.

The reason our clients tend to stay with us for so long is basic. We understand their needs. Miles and I were both clients before we got into this business and we had trouble working with agencies. Specifically, we couldn't reconcile the concept of billable hours and retainers, paying for meetings, paying for proposals, paying for travel time, paying to bring three people to a meeting, paying to be invoiced, and paying to reconcile the budget. We felt we were always being ripped off, and we always had to ask for justification of the charges at the end of every month.

When we started the agency together, it was interesting to discover we both felt this way. So our model was to quote everything at a flat rate, and we didn't charge for all of those many other things I just listed. There was never a meter running.

When our clients were presented with this idea, they said they had never heard it before. They loved it, because they were so sick of the budgetary confrontation with their agency every single month.

Working flat rate enables everybody in the agency to do a better job. The creative director is never told he/she has only five hours to spend on a project and warned not to go over. After all, that's counterproductive to the way a creative brain works, and it means a hard stop when they hit their five hours. Ultimately the client doesn't get the best work possible.

But you also need to keep a lens focused on the bottom line. You need information. You must have a financial infrastructure in place. We still do a P&L on every single project, including monthly financial statements, monthly cash flow forecasts, and monthly sales forecasts. We're never surprised. We always know what our financial position is, and I think most small businesses don't.

This is a crucial mistake, because without this information you don't know when you should reduce or increase your staff, reduce or increase your office space, reduce your expenses, reduce your salaries, reduce management salaries, reduce your benefits, improve your cash flow, reduce or increase your pricing, reduce or increase your profit margins, or renegotiate with your bank. You won't have the power to do any of these things.

Something else I've learned is when you're making money in good times, you don't rape your company and take out your retained earnings. Leave it there. Leave your investment in your company. If you have to draw down on your retained earnings in tough times, then that's what you do. Just don't operate hand-to-mouth. And be sure to rely on your accountant for proper tax planning.

Also, we've always worked to act ethically toward our employees. It's important from a humanistic standpoint; we should all treat each other well. And one of the luxuries of being a small or medium-sized business is that owners are able to treat their staff as colleagues, with humanity, when big companies usually don't. Miles and I both came from huge companies where we were both a number, and no one wants to be treated that way.

I am proud to say many of our employees have been here 10 or more years, a few even 15 years. We have a high retention rate and very low turnover. I would hope that 90 per cent of the people who have worked here, but left, would say there was something about their experience here that was worthwhile, that they learned something, and that the people who work here are decent—because life is just too short. I'm proud to say I still have friendships with people who were here 10 or 15 years ago.

As you know now, my background before this business was in sales, and the biggest thrill for somebody with a sales background is typically the win. For some it's the hunt, but not me. For me it's the win. Every time we win a new client it's a huge thrill, because these days it takes a long time to land a new client. The phone doesn't ring off the hook the way it used to, because the climate isn't like that in our industry anymore.

We have to seek out new opportunities, and that's fine, but we also have more competition. And there's much more reticence on behalf of clients to switch agencies. They're scared; they don't have time and they're afraid of the unknown (the devil they know is better than the one they don't).

It can take a year or more to win a new client, but for me it's a huge thrill every time because I know that we've worked hard for it and that they have confidence we'll do the job. The second greatest thrill after we've won a client happens when we do the first big project for them and they say they've never worked with anyone like us—and not only in Canada; it's when the U.S. folks that the Canadians report to shake their heads and say, "Wow, this agency is unbelievable." Those are my two biggest thrills, and I still experience them 20 years later.

Still, it's not an endless stream of thrills.

The last five years have been personally challenging, probably even more so than after the tech bubble burst. Our industry now, both the technology industry we serve and the marketing industry, is much more mature. For a while I felt the nature of what we do, in many cases, had become repetitive and commoditized and not particularly exciting. We did good work, we had good clients, but it became kind of a treadmill for me personally. A year and a half ago something happened to absolutely flip a switch in me and that was social media.

Suddenly, as a direct marketer, I saw an entirely new world open up. I still don't think we fully understand it or have our arms around it, but I'm so excited to have something to sink my teeth into again and to get my brain working in a way that it hasn't in a really long time.

Sometimes I feel really overwhelmed. It's like drinking through a fire hose. It's what wakes me up in the middle of the night, not in a bad way, in a really exciting way. But also in a way that, as somebody who has hit the half-century mark, makes me feel like I'm running out of time and I have to really hurry to get this.

That's not a bad thing. I've put more pressure on myself than I have in a long time, but I actually do better under pressure. That's what motivates me: figuring out ways to deliver new services to our clients that get better results, using everything in our power—and now that includes social media. While my issues around control have abated somewhat, my passion for providing unparalleled MarCom services to clients, for technology, and for my agency have never been so strong.

8

GROWTH DOESN'T GUARANTEE SURVIVAL

How Becoming Better, Leaner Managers Lets Us Succeed

ROBERT MILLS & RAY MILLS
Co-founders, Kudu Industries Inc.

(From left) Ray Mills and Robert Mills

"Don't become so absorbed in working *in* the business that you fail to work *on* the business."

ROBERT MILLS & RAY MILLS

TYPE OF BUSINESS: *Pump manufacturer, oil industry* | FOUNDED: *Calgary, Alberta, 1989*

www.kudupump.com

WHAT DOES IT TAKE FOR A BIG BUSINESS TO SURVIVE a severe economic downturn? Find out in this lesson-packed story from Robert and Ray.

ROBERT: In 1977 I had the misfortune of being part owner and operator of some heavy oil wells near Lloydminster, Alberta. People thought they represented a great opportunity because it was so easy to find these heavy oil formations. They were right, but nobody wanted this opportunity because a lot of sand is produced when pumping such heavy, tarry oil. Since sand is abrasive, it was wrecking pumps and causing numerous delays. We were losing a tonne of money.

While trying to come up with a solution, I became aware of a type of pump called a progressing cavity pump (PCP) being used in tank trucks to move sandy oil. But no one was making a progressing cavity pump for an oil well.

My production foreman had worked for Husky Oil and was aware of an experiment Husky had done with a Russian PCP. The Russians ran the pump in the well with an electrical submersible motor. It worked too well. The motor rotated the pump at 3,600 rpm, ran the well dry in 15 minutes, and burned out the pump. But the technology showed potential.

Husky Oil had patented the idea of putting a planetary gear speed reducer between the electrical submersible motor and the pump, but they never developed it.

This was my way in. I started working on a way to drive a PCP on the bottom of a well using a mechanical drive from the surface. I didn't want to use an expensive electrical submersible motor like the Russian group did, and I didn't want wires in the well making workovers complicated. I came up with the idea of rotating the production tubing all the way down the well to rotate the rotor of the PCP pump.

Two years later, in 1979, an engineer from California showed up in Canada. He had been trying to use PCPs in wells for some time and he picked an Edmonton company as his distributor. There were problems.

The pumps were being made by a rubber moulder who was inexperienced with this type of pump. The moulder had trouble gluing the elastomer to the steel casing, which is absolutely critical. The pumps weren't reliable, and his entire system was designed for shallow stripper wells anyway; large companies couldn't make money with them.

But oil companies in Canada quickly recognized this technology was the answer to a major problem they had struggled with for 50 years. In fact, today Canada is the only place in the world where heavy oil is produced with large amounts of sand. Elsewhere it's ignored. If they can't screen out the sand, they don't produce it.

Unfortunately for me, the Edmonton-based distributor for the Californian engineer got a German PCP manufacturer to design pumps for oil wells, and developed the business rapidly.

I plodded on with my drive system but didn't get very far, until 1988. A French company had heard about the Russian experiment with the submersible PCP and saw the potential too. They had designed oil-well pumps, and I asked to be the Canadian distributor for their equipment, so I could marry their pump with my drive system.

RAY: My dad and I decided to form a company to distribute the French company's pumps, while fine-tuning my dad's tubing drive pumping system as an add-on. We pooled our savings, founded Kudu Industries Inc., and began work out of our garage.

But when we hit the streets to sell the pumps with my dad's drive system, almost nobody was interested. A year after an initial two-pump sale, we were no further ahead.

By late September of 1989, we only had those two test units out in the field. We had exhausted our savings and our credit cards were maxed out. Things were looking pretty bleak. No one wanted to take a chance on us, and we had failed to raise any money to get the company moving forward.

We'd been persistent, and the few pumps were running extremely well, but customers have to run these pumps for months to determine whether it is an improvement over the old one. With that kind of timeline, we didn't know if we would survive long enough to find out.

Finally, in early October of 1989, Renaissance Energy, a customer testing one of the pumps, called up and told us they were impressed. They ordered 10 more units. This was a complete shock, but an incredibly welcome one.

ROBERT: Ray was doing all the field work at this time. We started off with a different business model than the two established companies, which were selling through supply stores. Supply stores just plop products on their shelves. They don't do much of a sales job. They don't support customers by offering technical support or service.

Ray delivered right to the well site and we sold directly to the oil companies. He discovered that the service rigs didn't know how to install the pumps properly. We made sure our pumps were installed properly, so of course they worked a lot better.

This allowed us to open up a new market that wasn't crowded by the two existing suppliers. We could also prove the superiority of our business model. The two competitors were eventually forced to copy us.

We started opening service centres in the field. The others did too, but I think we did a much better job of training our people to better support our clients. We've always seen ourselves as a service company, and our model has always been to make our customers successful.

It didn't work everywhere. In the U.S., this technology was completely discounted. Our two established competitors went to the U.S. before we did. They didn't test the pumps before running them in wells that were higher in temperature than those in Canada. They didn't get the fit between the components right. It was a disaster. The technology still has not been accepted for pumping oil wells in the U.S. We eventually gave up there because our time was better spent in overseas markets.

RAY: In Canada, installing and servicing the pumps at Renaissance Energy initially represented more than 80 per cent of our business. We were scrambling just to keep up with their demand. At the time, Renaissance was by far the busiest driller in Canada. When they saw how well our pumps worked, within a space of six months we were doing most of their business. We almost didn't have time to look for other customers.

This was a dramatic turnaround for us. Quickly the five-year plan my dad and I had developed went out the window because, based on Renaissance's business alone, we'd exceeded our growth objectives.

When people saw how well Renaissance was doing with our pumps, we were able to build on that success. Renaissance was revolutionary in the way it produced wells. This was enabled by the pumps we had at the time, which changed how pumped wells were produced. When other players adopted Renaissance's methodology, it catapulted our growth.

Many of our customers already had pumping systems into which we adapted our pump. And from this point forward we would see shortcomings in other people's equipment, and we eventually began to design entire systems. In fact, that's where my dad spent the majority of his time initially; he was designing the components we didn't have, so we could have them manufactured. By late 1990 we were able to put together entire systems. In fact, we installed the first complete Kudu PCP system on my 25th birthday.

Personally, I was thrilled to be in a business that was making money after the start we'd had. I grew up in the oil patch and I was always interested in what my dad did, particularly when he was designing an innovative system for artificial lifts. I was involved from the outset, helping him with drawings and then assembling the system in our garage as he built prototypes.

When the opportunity came to work with Dad, I was coming to the end of a work contract and the timing was perfect. It was a natural fit. We both had an entrepreneurial bent and Dad had run his own companies for years. I did go to engineering school, but I didn't finish. I was ready to get out there, and my mind is scientifically/mathematically focused.

But this didn't prepare me for sales. If you ask any entrepreneur what is the one thing they are poorest at, nine times out of 10 they'll probably say sales, and the worst thing about sales is cold calling. I just had to power through and stick with it, understanding it was normal to make 10 phone calls for every one I'd get back.

Meanwhile, we were always undercapitalized. When you have rapid growth, you sometimes struggle to cover the spread between your receivables and your payables. It was really tough at first to finance our growth. We really had to cajole customers to pay as quickly as possible. This was a huge challenge.

We had other challenges, the biggest in 1998 when the price of oil collapsed, dropping to less than $10 a barrel. In our case we almost didn't make it through the downturn. I know it sounds dramatic, but it actually came down to a matter of hours. We call this our near-death experience.

When oil hit $10 a barrel our business literally dropped to zero in about half the markets we served. We had to rapidly contract. We went from 110 employees to 55, and of the 10 service stations we had at the time, we closed half.

People thought we were overreacting. Many of our customers were actually hostile about how quickly we contracted, saying it was premature and we were compromising our ability to service them. I suppose in some cases they were right, but it was a matter of survival.

We made the hard cuts, and it was extremely painful. By 1998 we already had a nicely sized little company with great people working for us. We had to say goodbye to many of those people, which was very difficult. But it wasn't the hardest part.

Though we had started cutting, ultimately the bank showed up and told us we were insolvent. The fact that we had an offer on the table to buy our company was the only thing that kept them at bay. It bought us some time, and during this time we each prepared for a different possible outcome. My dad tried to save the company and arrange alternate financing, while I tried to sell the company as best I could.

Although my dad and I had spent enough years in the oil industry and knew downturns happened, we had failed to plan appropriately. We'd grown too quickly. We'd grown beyond our ability to manage the company effectively. We were making a lot of mistakes, but we kind of dismissed them as the unavoidable downside of speedy growth. However, failing to manage the company as well as we should have put us in a real bind when oil prices went south.

We were also managing too much. We thought we were allowing people to make important decisions but in reality we weren't. We hadn't prepared them for such decisions, but these decisions were still ending up on our desks. Ultimately this would have limited the growth of the company, but at the time it was hindering how the company was managed.

We didn't have a lot of the systems, processes, and procedures in place we should have. It came down to our own lack of training and experience in running a company this size. I guess we thought we had learned enough through osmosis but our debt was too high, our inventories were too high, and our inventory turns were too low.

When we looked back at the results over the two or three years prior to the downturn, we should have seen the warning signs. Even when you're growing, if your profit is eroding at some point, the two lines are going to cross; you'll be a growing company that's losing money. We were ignoring this while pedalling as fast as we could.

In the course of trying to save or sell the company, our survival came down to a matter of a few hours. We secured new financing the morning of our final meeting to sell Kudu.

The other company had done its due diligence and the oil patch had continued to deteriorate, so we were pretty sure the offer they were going to put forward would be much lower than the original offer. Kudu, and the industry as a whole, was hurting.

So Dad and I sat down together to talk it out. We suddenly had new financing and a huge decision to make. We figured we'd at least stemmed the bleeding because, while we still weren't making any money, we were losing less and less each day. We asked each other whether we should continue on and trust we'd turned the corner—or should we consider the final offer?

In the end, we decided on a minimum price above which we'd sell and below which we'd use the new financing to keep Kudu going.

I remember it like it was yesterday. We went into the meeting with the acquiring company and their final offer was what we thought it would be: a small fraction of the original offer. So we politely said no and walked out of their boardroom.

There was complete stunned silence on their part. They knew we were in trouble and they came in with a low-ball final offer. I couldn't blame them, it was just business. But it did hurt a bit. When we walked out that boardroom I said to my dad, "I guess we're moving forward."

There was still no certainty at all. There was still plenty of risk. I remember getting in my truck on that day in June of 1998 and sitting there for some time, thinking, "My God! What have I gotten myself into?"

It was around this time that we made a transformative change in the way we operated.

My dad met a fellow from the Industrial Research Assistance Program (IRAP), part of the National Research Council, and he introduced us to "lean manufacturing." The core idea behind lean is to maximize customer value while minimizing waste. The ultimate goal is to provide perfect value to the customer through a perfect value-creation process that has zero waste. Eliminating waste along entire value streams, instead of at isolated points, creates processes that need less human effort, less space, less capital, and less time.

We really saw a new way to manage the company. It would give us the tools to empower our employees to help them manage better. It would help us turn Kudu into the kind of company that could compete in the marketplace.

It worked. In our darkest days we had been insolvent with a debt of about $9 million and $13 million in inventory, turning our inventory less than twice a year. People always worry that if you don't have enough inventory you lose sales. Well, at a record amount of inventory in 1997, we lost 250 sales due to stock-outs. By 2003 we'd reduced it to five lost sales due to stock-outs for the year. We did this with two-thirds less inventory. By the end of 2003 we had zero debt and our inventory turns were six times a year. We were paying bonuses. We subsequently made three acquisitions.

We applied lean to manufacturing, then distribution. Within the last couple of years we've started applying it across the company, and it is now in place in our back office. Probably the last thing to get the lean treatment will be our accounting department—but even accounting has already been touched by it.

Besides being far more efficient, the near-death experience taught us to watch our numbers closely. We were a bit blasé, thinking they would take care of themselves as long as the sales were rolling in the door.

We became very cautious about accounts receivable, relearning how to chase outstanding money and remembering people don't just pay us out of a sense of obligation. We became more disciplined about some of our supplier relationships. Finally, we began thinking more strategically about our company, after having loosely put together budgets and plans for many years.

*   *   *

As we reflected on what we learned in late 1999 and early 2000, we rejected diversifying our product line outside of our core business, partially because of our lean experience. But we diversified our markets. We started looking outside of Canada, into countries like Russia, Romania, Kazakhstan, Oman, and Australia.

Entering new markets was exciting because it was tough. It required a lot of new knowledge and problem solving. It was like a lot of other big business challenges I've always enjoyed, whether technical, financial, or customer-related. When I've wrestled hard with an idea or challenge for a long time and then something suddenly twigs and someone nails a solution—those are moments I truly treasure.

I also get a huge kick out of seeing our team get excited about Kudu. When you help people, through training, mentoring, or coaching, to get better at their jobs and they show enthusiasm, it's incredibly fulfilling.

As are big sales wins. But when we made our first big sale in 1989 to Renaissance, I'll admit we didn't have much time to celebrate. I remember we laughed with great relief, but it didn't last long because then we really had to scramble to support the demand.

This may sound strange, but it's both tough and critically important as an entrepreneur to properly celebrate successes. Often we're too wrapped up in the moment to acknowledge them and don't give them their due. Sometimes we forget it's not just about us—we have to share successes with the rest of the people we work with. And you don't necessarily need to throw a big party. You can go out for dinner or cocktails. You just need to take the time to stop and acknowledge everyone who contributed to a big win. Then you can move forward.

Of course this same acknowledgement should go to an entrepreneur's family members as well, since they can sometimes bear the brunt of some highly stressful days. I know this from experience.

I always thought I didn't take work home because I tried to not talk about it. I also tried not to worry about it. But, in the mornings shortly after I got up, probably at some point during or after my shower, I was putting on my business game face.

I didn't realize how much of an effect this had on my family until I did a personality test about eight years ago. I brought the results home to share them because I'd never done one before. My kids read it and they laughed, and my sharing this with them made them feel comfortable sharing with me. While they don't think of things in these terms, they said, "Dad that's you. Now we understand that when you leave the house with that face in the morning it's not because you're mad at us, it's because you're already thinking about work and your challenges." I had no idea I was leaving the house with my game face on and that everybody was on pins and needles. We laughed about it, but I guess I can look like I'm about to tear somebody's head off! It really impacted the family.

Shortly after, I had a business consultant working at Kudu who pointed out the same thing. She said, "You know, Ray, when you're walking around the company you don't realize the impact you're having." When I asked her what she meant, she said, "You've got this look on your face. I know you, I know you're not upset and I know you're just thinking, but the look on your face is very, very serious. When you walk by, people think you're upset about something."

I often stopped and talked to people in a relaxed way, so I figured people knew I wasn't upset. But, of course, I didn't talk to everybody. She told me I tend to leave behind a pretty high wake. She advised me if there was nothing bothering me, I should look happy. I took this to heart.

I've made certain other changes as well.

As a result, work is different now. My position has evolved. By now I've sometimes reluctantly delegated some of the tasks that at one time I loved to do. It was part of our turnaround plan. Luckily, in most cases I've found new things to do and found enjoyment in those. But my job doesn't get any easier. One challenge is to stay motivated, and it's closely linked to constantly trying to do things better, in both good and bad times.

I've talked to other business owners who were better prepared than we were when we hit the market downturn and oil price drop. I've learned a few things we could do differently next time to improve, but it's exhausting coming out of it. I'm really enjoying how busy we are today trying to keep up with business again, but those things do take their toll. It was exhausting to try to keep everybody motivated and working to have a good attitude.

I challenged just about every executive or business person I knew on what we could do better next time and not one person could tell me. Everybody nods and says it's important to get ready and act quickly, but nobody really knows how to do it.

The bottom line is that it's about staying profitable and keeping people motivated. This to me is the real measure of how to stay profitable. How do you maintain morale? How do you keep people positive? Those are the things I want to accomplish when the next downturn comes.

You have to spend time on the business. Don't ignore it. Don't become so absorbed *in* working in the business that you fail to work *on* the business.

Also, I know if we had started using lean principles from the get-go we would have done better. There's nothing better than seeing employees succeed, and lean makes this happen often at Kudu. And, besides learning to delegate better, lean thinking is allowing me to spend more time with my family. This is a very good thing.

ROBERT: For me, one of the highs at Kudu actually came in 1998, when we implemented lean and conformed to the ISO 9001-2000 standard to turn the company around. ISO 9001 is the internationally recognized standard for the quality management of businesses. It applies to the processes that create and control the products and services an organization supplies, prescribes control of activities to ensure the expectations of customers are met, and is designed to apply to virtually any product or service, made by any process anywhere in the world.

After we started putting lean manufacturing in place, one of the guys on the shop floor came to me and asked me when the layoffs would start. I was taken aback because I hadn't been thinking in those terms. He pointed out that with lean manufacturing we wouldn't need as many people. I thought for a moment and I said, "Well that's right, but we're not going to need as much space either." We actually found we had 30 per cent more workspace. Until that time we'd contracted out all our machining. I told the employee that we would buy machine tools and do our own machining.

That's what we did. We started training people to be machinists on our newly freed-up floor space. We not only retained all those people, but also we hired more. It was a real thrill.

We then put in a program to train journeymen welders and what are now referred to as industrial mechanics (formerly millwrights and stationary engineers). We also train heavy duty mechanics. We keep them on full pay when they do their three months of school work every year during their apprenticing, and this has really built a lot of employee loyalty. The people on our shop floor have a list of relatives who want to come to work for us so they can eventually learn one of these skill sets.

I definitely recommend lean manufacturing, along with ISO for quality; the two go very well together. But to make them really effective you have to be willing to delegate responsibilities and decision making. I think we've done a good job of this. A lot of people on our shop floor now have company credit cards in their pockets, and if a supplier shows up at the back door equipped to swipe a credit card, for example, he is paid immediately. Two of the team leaders order hundreds of thousands of dollars worth of equipment a week. Nobody checks their work. All of our purchasing is done right off the shop floor and the people have a simple way to control inventory.

It's been an important transition. Before, almost every decision had to come from Ray or myself. Today I'm chairman of the board and strictly play an advisory role. But don't get me wrong. I'm still working, motivated, and happy. Kudu is my baby and I still get excited about it. I don't see that ever changing.

9

THE SLINGSHOT EFFECT

How Gaining Ample Expertise First Can Pay Dividends in the Long Run

GERHARD RAUCH

Co-founder, Helton Industries

(*From left*) Gerhard Rauch and Henry Neels

"One of the most important things we learned early on was to stay on top of our receivables. The longer they were outstanding, the harder it was to collect them."

GERHARD RAUCH

TYPE OF BUSINESS: *Manufacturer of overhead door products* | FOUNDED: *Abbotsford, British Columbia, 1981*
www.heltonindustries.com

WHEN I EMIGRATED FROM GERMANY TO CANADA in 1966 with a degree in mechanical engineering, my entrepreneurial nature was already evident. My father passed away when I was 7 years old and, as a result, I needed to become more independent than other children my age. I took care of my younger twin siblings from quite early on, helping my mother make ends meet during challenging times in post-war Germany.

I led an entrepreneur's life as a young person, doing jobs like landscape maintenance, decorating, and painting. After completing a machinist apprenticeship, I studied mechanical engineering. As a young person I frequently used my skills to design and invent. I came up with unique ways to customize cars and motorcycles that I owned, creating prototypes that could have been commercially produced.

It would still be some time before I would get to call the shots in a business I created, but I knew one day I wanted to make this a reality.

About 15 years after arriving in Canada and after years of preparation, I actually used many of my father's original hand tools when my partner Henry Neels and I first started our business, Helton Industries. This symbolic act brought back many memories. I wish I could give my father a tour of Helton's plant today.

My father had always dreamed of owning his own machine shop. Now it was my dream.

*   *   *

I worked for two different Canadian companies before consulting from home during 1973 and 1974. While providing mechanical design and drafting services to several local companies, my entrepreneurial desire intensified.

In 1974, I designed various metal forming machines for a local company that then offered me a well-paying position. I put my entrepreneurial dreams on hold and instead worked at their offices for seven years as a mechanical design engineer and vice-president.

Ultimately, it turned out to be a fortunate turn of events, since this is where I met Henry Neels, who has been my business partner ever since we incorporated Helton in 1981.

Henry had been employed at the company since 1969. A machinist apprentice, he had also supervised the machine shop prior to his journeyman exam and had been promoted to production manager. Henry and I always worked well as a team, designing and manufacturing unique metal forming machines. We often discussed my machine designs. Henry's exceptional hands-on and practical talents always complemented my design work. I always valued his opinion.

During my seven years with the company, I visited many customers and set up new machines, helping them jump-start new business ventures, some good, some bad. I continued to gather knowledge about potential products, requirements, and customers.

The old craving resurfaced. I kept thinking of how, at all my previous positions, I had put in my best effort, as if I had been working for my own company. Several times I was even offered 10 to 15 per cent shareholder equity to join other firms, but I always declined. I could see myself doing most of the work without being able to make any important business decisions.

At last, near the end of 1980, I decided to cut the harnesses associated with employee life to start on my own journey. I looked forward to the personal challenges, satisfaction, and financial rewards. At the age of 40, these had become higher priorities.

I discussed my plans confidentially with Henry. Coincidentally, he also planned to quit in 1981 to start his own business. Whereas Henry thought he might pursue a business in the farming industry, after some discussion we decided to combine our talents and start a rollformed product manufacturing business. We agreed on 50/50 ownership.

Although Henry was 14 years younger, the age difference didn't bother me. It never has. I always felt younger than my real age—and I still do today at 70.

We soon decided to name the new company HELTON—a combination of the first three letters of my wife's name, Helga, and Henry's wife's name, Tona.

In order to respect our current employer, we made sure the new venture didn't interfere with our employee responsibilities. During January and February 1981, we designed our rollforming line during weekends and on many weekday evenings.

Rollforming is a progressive process that passes a metal strip through a series of specially shaped roller dies to ultimately form a desired rollformed profile. Strip stock is fed through successive pairs of contoured rolls that progressively form the work piece to meet the desired specifications. We purchased machines such as lathes and milling machines to build the rollforming line. However, in order to minimize costs, materials for building the line were purchased from surplus metal and salvage dealers.

In March 1981, we started building the rollforming line in my garage. Only our immediate families were aware of our plans. By the end of August 1981 the line was completed and we handed in our resignations.

When we told people what we planned to do, we received a lot of negative feedback: Do you really know what you are doing? How can you just give up solid employment and a steady income? The economy isn't strong; this is the worst possible time to start a business. Be responsible and think of your family's future.

In fact, these types of comments made us more determined to succeed. Neither Henry nor I believed in letting others dampen our enthusiasm. If you have conviction in your ideas, we thought, you should drive them forward with all your might. We'd driven forward the ideas of others for far too long.

Looking back, I think starting our business during a down economy helped us. We were forced to keep overheads extremely low and manufacturing efficiencies high. Also, our competitors were struggling to shed expenses while we were small, nimble, and able to operate frugally.

During August and September 1981, we signed a lease for a 4,300-square-foot warehouse in Abbotsford, B.C., halfway between Henry's house and mine. Helton Industries was incorporated.

In October, we built a 400-square-foot office inside the corner of the warehouse, bought an old three-wheel forklift, and moved all our machines into the warehouse. To keep costs down, we did all the work ourselves with used desks, drawing boards, and filing cabinets taken from our homes.

It was time to seek funding. We put together cash flow projections and applied for a line of credit at a local bank but were declined, mainly because of negative experiences they'd had with other manufacturing companies. Also, they didn't understand the particular type of business we were starting. I remember the bank manager saying it would be easier to get financing for a fast-food outlet.

We were warned that even if we had a solid relationship with a bank in good times, if things were to begin to go badly, their attitude could change drastically.

During the recession of 1981, interest rates were above 21 per cent, inflation was around 12.5 per cent, and unemployment was close to 8 per cent. Banks were extremely careful about lending money. We had arranged for mortgages on our homes prior to starting our business. These funds were our "standby line of credit." Fortunately, we never had to use them.

A year or two later we switched to another bank where they gave us a line of credit we hardly ever used. The original bank found out about the other bank and tried to get us to come back. At this point, our company was carrying no other loans.

In the 1980s banks sometimes looked down on their clientele, whereas today they have a little more appreciation for the business they are getting. At that time you kind of had to hold your hat in your hand.

We weren't prepared to beg. But we were prepared to work hard—on anything. While designing and manufacturing our own tooling for our products, we took on any type of designing, machining, or welding work. We designed and built a tulip bulb planter and built trailer hitches. We repaired a garbage compactor and we did custom machining of various parts.

Our spouses worked with us to keep costs low. For example, we had a small punch press at our homes to do custom work. Even our children were involved with the operation, doing various assembly, light manufacturing, and janitorial jobs.

During the first year, we produced our first rollformed products, including highway delineator posts, reinforcing struts for overhead doors, and perforated angles (angled metal with a series of punched holes used to hang garage door tracks and garage door openers). We came up with high-speed manufacturing processes, such as punching eighty 3/8-inch diameter holes per second, spaced 1 inch apart in 1/8-inch-thick steel. With such specialized processes, we could offer our products at competitive prices.

Potential customers in the garage door industry liked our first products and asked if we had plans to manufacture other hardware items, including door tracks, hinges, brackets, and mounting angles. So we focused on these products and purchased additional machinery like punch presses and benders for which we made our own tooling. We developed high-speed automated tooling to keep quality high and costs low.

Initially we had to place orders for steel coils with local service centres. Ordering directly from steel mills was not possible; it required larger quantities, and the mills did not want to compete with their customers—many of whom were service centres.

In order to offer competitive pricing, we concentrated on efficient production methods and tolerated lower profit margins. We knew one day we would order our materials directly from steel mills and see improved profits. (To put this in perspective, in the early days it took considerable effort to purchase a 3,000-pound steel coil, while today it is not uncommon to purchase 6 million pounds of steel at a time.)

At this time, Henry and I also began to specialize in our respective roles internally. Henry concentrated on production and operations, and I focused my efforts on business development and sales. We both had similar involvement in machinery and tooling design, and we both knew the best way to drive the business forward was to capitalize on our key strengths.

One of the most important things we learned early on was to stay on top of our receivables. The longer they were outstanding, the harder it was to collect them. We paid special attention to this issue because we had seen slow-paying customers put plenty of small companies out of business over the years.

To ensure we got paid, we invoiced promptly and made sure our customers adhered to our terms. Sometimes we'd have to call. And sometimes they weren't in. So, knowing their vehicles, and seeing them parked in their lot, we just kind of dropped by without an invitation. Then we'd threaten to stay until we got a cheque. I think many of these customers respected our fortitude. In many cases these cheques were already made out and in the bottom drawer. They were just holding them as long as they could. The squeaky wheel gets the grease.

Expanding in Western Canada and entering U.S. markets was our next challenge. Helton was completely unknown in many of these markets, and there were large, well-established competitors.

At the time I thought maybe my heavy German accent might be hampering our sales. People often asked my nationality. After a while, I developed what I thought was a clever response: "I'm Canadian," I said with a smile. Interestingly, more than one person reflected on my answer and offered a sincere, "I thought so." I believe now my accent was actually a benefit, since it distinguished me from others in our industry.

Maybe it helped lead to our first major win. I can still vividly recall the personal satisfaction Henry and I felt upon delivering our first 20,000-linear-foot order of perforated angle to a very large garage door wholesaler in the American Pacific Northwest. We made sure we serviced the account very well, and in the following years became their main supplier for many more products.

During the first few years, we concentrated on supplying large overhead door companies that ordered full truckload orders only (45,000 lbs). We later diversified to sell to smaller customers who required shorter lead times and higher levels of customer service.

Although the larger customers pressured Helton not to sell to others, particularly smaller dealers, we managed their requests by providing them with extremely competitive volume pricing. From the fewer than 10 customers we had during the first few years, Helton now supplies more than 300 door manufacturers and dealers.

*　　*　　*

One of our greatest accomplishments came in 1988 when we launched Westgate Door, our wholesale distribution division. Originally we were selling much of our overhead door hardware for local markets through a distribution centre owned by a competitor of Helton's that produced its own hardware. But, after their head office mandated they purchase hardware internally, we formed Westgate Door, and the majority of their employees and customers came to us.

Westgate's sales were substantial in the first month, and the business is still flourishing today with locations throughout Western Canada. The competing distribution centre was closed down within a year due to a lack of business.

We attribute our success with Westgate and Helton to certain key tenets of our philosophy, the most important of which are business ethics and integrity. We encourage all our employees to exhibit these values. Henry and I have sons in the business who have worked for Helton for almost 20 years. It's nice to see that together they are continuing Helton's important moral leadership. This is critical when it comes to developing and maintaining customer relationships.

In our business there are tight timelines; many customers want their order yesterday, so you have to accurately promise delivery dates. We have a scheduling agenda for engineering and all projects, and every week we check their status. This way we know, with precision, what we are doing, as well as which resources are available when we're asked to start something new.

But the unexpected does happen. In the rare instance that we are late, we are always upfront with the customers. We don't give false excuses like "It's in transit" or "Raw materials didn't arrive in time." If those statements are not true, if you lie to customers and they find out, they'll never take you seriously again.

In the same way, we value honest business practices in others. If these qualities are not there, we'd rather not deal with them.

For example, in 1998, while on a Canadian government-sponsored economic mission to China, we signed a tentative partnership agreement with a large Chinese company.

Having the gut feeling this company might only be interested in copying our technology, I watered down the agreement to make it less definite. My inclination was correct. After their president, chief engineer, and marketing manager visited our plant, their members called one of our programmable logic controller (PLC) suppliers and asked if the supplier could build the same manufacturing machine for them. Our supplier said no and told us about the solicitation. We immediately ended our relationship with the Chinese company.

Besides reinforcing our need to deal with other honest businesspeople, this experience taught us to keep certain key processes confidential.

It was also clear we needed a solution to compete with Chinese imports. Other manufacturers and distributors were importing offshore products and to some degree it was displacing our business. In order to compete with Asian imports, we developed shorter lead times and minimal quantity restrictions so our customers were not required to carry large inventories.

Initially we imported some of the low-cost components through a broker in order to remain competitive. However, we noticed that quality was difficult to maintain and pricing was not consistently competitive. Therefore, we have expanded our Asian sourcing to include a full-time employee in China who buys raw materials and complementary products to those we manufacture. Through this office we also monitor the quality and packaging prior to shipping. These are high-volume hardware items, purchased at the best prices.

There are also pricing and cost issues to keep a close eye on when exporting to the U.S. The value of the Canadian currency vs. the U.S. currency has a significant effect on any Canadian manufacturer. Throughout the period 2000–2010, the value of the U.S. dollar declined by approximately 45 per cent. Since Helton's main customer base is in the U.S. and products are sold in U.S. dollars, this decline has had a great impact on revenues. Fortunately, most raw materials are purchased in U.S. dollars and so is a majority of Westgate's inventory, so the impact on Helton was minimized. In addition, Westgate's sales in Canada are growing, so there was little negative impact on our business. This geographical and business diversification was, and still is, a key component in helping us stay financially strong.

Recently, Helton expanded product lines to include accessory items such as weather seal, door lubricants, and additional access controls. We also set up divisions to manufacture window products and torsion springs for garage doors. The addition of these product categories took Helton one step closer to our goal of becoming a single source of supply for most of our customers.

In 2010 and 2011 Helton acquired two overhead door companies that provide complete installation and service of overhead doors and entry systems in their respective markets. These acquisitions provide further vertical integration and mean the Helton group of companies has representation in five different locations in British Columbia, two in Alberta, and one in Saskatchewan.

We know we're doing well from a financial perspective, but there are other achievements that are equally important.

Employees are the most critical asset of any business. Helton makes sure our employees feel valued, respected, and appreciated. We create an open culture where communication between all levels of the business is encouraged. This creates a happy and productive work environment. We like the idea of our employees going home at night and saying, "I like my job."

We believe companies should have a strong HR manager with good, two-way, trusting relationships with employees. We have an employee team specifically dedicated to employee concerns. We call this our HEAT (Helton Employee Action Team). Its focus is to ensure there is a good communication channel between employees and senior management.

Our monthly newsletter is a good tool for informing employees of company activities, honouring employee achievements, and monitoring successes of various teams for improving the workplace and production performance.

As an owner you must always have an open-door policy and welcome employees to share their thoughts or concerns with you. Let your employees know they are part of the team just like you are, and make sure you set a good example. Always remember, people work for people—not companies. A good rapport is essential.

We have believed this from day one. We have actually been proven correct several times. For example, four employees from the company where Henry and I were co-workers joined us soon after we started. More recently, Helton's employees rejected unionization with a strong majority vote.

Henry and I received a distinguished service award from the International Door Association in 2007, an association with 300 manufacturer and 1,700 dealer members worldwide. We both took great satisfaction from this industry acknowledgement.

Today Henry and I are still expanding our business, but we do look to the future sometimes and ask ourselves how long we might want to continue our active roles in the business. I am of retirement age and continue to have many other business and personal interests requiring my attention. Henry is younger at 55 and is involved with quite a few other business ventures. In fact, he runs a very successful dairy farm with one of his sons. Henry's other son is a successful member of our purchasing team, having worked at Helton for over 15 years.

Knowing we have established a highly capable leadership team led by my two sons gives me great satisfaction. This also makes it possible for me to spend more time managing my other investments and interests. Henry is still very active in the business and works there three to four days per week. I am so proud to see how well my sons work together with Henry.

My father would be proud too. I'm sure of it.

10
TAKING THE PLUNGE

From Potential Buyout Target to Real Estate Overachiever

VIVIAN RISI

Broker of Record, Royal LePage Your Community Realty

"It is imperative to remain adaptable and be prepared to weather storms."

VIVIAN RISI

TYPE OF BUSINESS: *Realtor* | FOUNDED: *Richmond Hill, Ontario, 1994*

www.yourcommunityrealty.com

FROM MY FIRST DAY IN REAL ESTATE, I HAD A VISION. I knew the real estate industry was where I wanted to be. I didn't know exactly how I was going to do it; I just knew I wanted to make a difference. I visualized a professional office environment that would offer realtors full service to help them excel, elevating them to success.

As a manager, I would attend meetings and listen to other managers talk about scaling down by cutting overhead and encouraging realtors to work from home. I did the opposite. I offered more services—such as training, coaching, and mentoring, among others—to enable my realtors to service their clients more effectively. I envisioned a company where realtors were happy to come into the office because they knew their success was at the forefront of my mind. I had a different vision.

I started out in the real estate industry at a young age in 1974, and even though my business soon began to flourish, I took time off to have a family and raise my three children. I returned to the industry in 1981 as a realtor with Canada Trust Realty and for 12 years was a top producer, despite interest rates of between 17 and 22 per cent, and other challenging market conditions. By May 1993, I was looking to move from sales into management. Since I had already been helping others increase their business, going into management seemed like a natural move. In addition, I was facing the challenge of being a single parent and looking for financial stability.

I enjoyed working in management. I thrived at nurturing people and helping them grow. Not only did I feel a strong obligation to ensure my realtors had all the necessary tools and support to succeed, this obligation fit with my initial vision: to be the best in the industry.

Six months into my new-found management role, my world of financial security was threatened. The company I worked with decided to merge with a large real estate firm and sell off its real estate division. This large real estate firm decided to franchise. It was going to sell all the newly acquired offices—including mine!

At the time, our small office was located in the community of York Region and consisted of 18 realtors. The chances of a new owner keeping me on as a manager were next to none. I would be looking for a new job. Panic set in. Things were changing so quickly I found myself in front of the most frightening decision of my life.

My financial security was gone. I could go back into sales but my passion was managing realtors, nurturing them, and encouraging them to grow into successful people. It is difficult to express exactly how I was feeling and thinking. Suffice it to say, I was overwhelmed. I came to the realization that the only security I could have was the security I would create for myself and for my children. I decided to take a huge leap of faith and buy the office.

I remembered that the president of Canada Trust Realty, during his announcement of the merger, had said, "Let us know if you are interested in buying any offices." His comment resounded in my head. Time stood still as I picked up the phone and made the call. I decided to stand; I knew I would feel more in control. I stood at my desk for the entire conversation! My timing was exactly right; he answered my call—and, to my surprise, he knew who I was. Within days I had met with the negotiating task force.

During my extensive meetings with them, I used my instincts, as well as every skill I had ever learned. After a few weeks and what seemed like an eternity, I negotiated one of the best "term deals" of my life. When we were signing the documents, one of my daughters was working at the front desk as a receptionist. She recalls one of the negotiators turning to her and commenting, "You are witnessing greatness in the making."

Then the reality set in. It was time to roll up my sleeves. I knew the company was losing money and I had my work cut out for me. I had to restructure, bring in more people, and reinvent the business. Thankfully, it didn't feel like an insurmountable goal. I simply took one step at a time. For the first time in my life I was in the driver's seat. Being free to run things my way gave me the confidence to realize my vision. I simply told myself, "You have no choice." I was bound and determined to make this work.

I made it my mandate to be at the leading edge by hiring people who could train and coach realtors. When it came to customer service, I wanted my realtors to stand out above all others. I incorporated a first-rate marketing department—this required capital, but it was worth the risk. By providing services so my agents could better service their customers, I'd create a chain reaction of positive experiences for both, and this would lead to mutual success.

Running a business and being a single parent was a difficult balancing act. I included my children by having both of my daughters help out at reception while my son ran a small cleaning company in the office. It was a nice way of keeping us together while retaining focus on the business. Even though their cleaning services weren't the best, having my teenage children involved in my business made it all worthwhile.

In the beginning, my greatest challenge came from competitors who were critical of what I was trying to achieve. They would do their best to plant uncertainty in the minds of my realtors. They'd say, "She can't do it" or, "She'll never be able to sustain it." Because I was a young, single parent and a female broker in a male-dominated industry, competitors did not waste opportunities to discredit me in any way they could.

In this industry, reputation is everything. I have always operated with integrity and respected my fellow realtors.

In addition, it was important for me to run an office where people felt good about coming in to work. Because I was facing challenges around rapid growth I learned a great many lessons. For example, having a solid business plan is essential. I was constantly reinvesting in my business. You would be hard pressed to find an entrepreneur who hasn't taken risks to grow his or her company.

Then, in 1999, I was introduced to Royal LePage by a business associate. During this meeting, I learned that Royal LePage was in the business of selling franchises. At the same time, they were offering to purchase my office. When I declined, Royal LePage offered to sell me three corporately owned offices in the vicinity of my current headquarters.

Fifteen years later my children have returned. After completing their education and obtaining degrees, they have joined my business as part of our executive management team. Today we are the largest franchise for Royal LePage in Canada, with more than 750 realtors spread across 11 offices.

I am grateful for the opportunity to be able to assist in the growth of my communities and I enjoy giving back to those communities. I sit on several local boards and contribute to more than 30 charities. One charity that is very dear to me supports and empowers women and children who live with domestic violence. A house is not a home unless it is safe.

When asked how I did it, I tell people I stayed on course, no matter what obstacles came my way. I never lost focus on my vision and my goals. Make no mistake; I have had my fair share of challenges. The key is to not get discouraged or thrown off track. When you are managing a large business there is no time to blink. You must take action swiftly; there is no time for hesitation. It is imperative to remain adaptable and be prepared to weather storms. This is especially true when the market is undergoing a major adjustment, as it did during the recession of the early 1990s or more recently in 2008 when our economy took a nose-dive and revenues were down by 50 per cent.

Like many other industries, we are a people industry. Listening to our clients' needs and being interested in them is essential to our success.

In fact, a concern I have about today's generation—with their cell phones, e-mailing, and plain-and-simple hiding behind a computer—is that they've lost the art of face-to-face communication. I'm always encouraging people to use technology to support their business. But they should use it as a tool and be cautious about letting it take over. People contact and eye contact are very important. I've seen a lot of realtors get caught up in constant texting and it's dangerous. You lose so much information when you don't see a person's response to a question or comment. You can't truly understand what a client is saying unless you're sitting directly across from them and picking up on their body language. A fax, e-mail, or text will never replace a face-to-face meeting.

As I reflect back on my career, I can summarize what I've learned through all my experiences with this personal motto: Never let anyone or anything stop you from being the person you are meant to be. Further, to find real success as an entrepreneur, you must stay true to yourself, keep your word, and work extremely hard. Not only do your clients and colleagues demand it, they deserve it. If you stay on this path, you are far more likely to be successful and content running your business, no matter what challenges may be thrown your way.

11
FROM AN IDEA TO AN EMPIRE

The Little Recycling Company That Could

LOUIS ANAGNOSTAKOS & TED MANZIARIS
Co-founders, Turtle Island Recycling

(*From left*) Louis Anagnostakos and Ted Manziaris

"Get off your ass and wear out a few pairs of shoes."

LOUIS ANAGNOSTAKOS & TED MANZIARIS

TYPE OF BUSINESS: *Recycling company* | FOUNDED: *Toronto, Ontario, 1991*

www.turtleislandrecycling.com

THIS IS HOW TWO FRIENDS, A VISION, AND A K-CAR GREW into a recognized brand by knowing what counts—relationships.

LOUIS: Does it always take a big break to turn an idea into a full-fledged entrepreneurial venture? I don't know, but without a doubt it's what happened to Ted Manziaris and me back in 1991 when our recycling and garbage collection business consisted of two guys and a beat-up K-car.

In those days we both had full-time jobs in other industries, but we used to hand out our Turtle Island business cards in Toronto during the day and collect scrap or trash at night. One Friday morning we dropped off our card with a guy named Bernie Fournier who was in charge of janitorial services at Maple Leaf Gardens. That night we got a phone call from him at around 11 P.M. Bernie said, "Look, I've got a problem. Do you guys have any trucks on the road?" I told him absolutely, and we'd be there in an hour.

The first obstacle was that Ted had the car because he was on a date with his girlfriend (now his wife). These were the days when a pager was considered leading edge. I paged Ted and he put his girlfriend on the bus and came to pick me up. He was in downtown Toronto and I lived in the east end.

Bernie told us that Maple Leaf Gardens was full of trash and there was no one to clean it up. The Gardens couldn't use the incinerator because the environment minister had banned incineration. The next day the facility was going to be hosting the Toronto Maple Leafs' most important charity event—the Bobby Orr Skate-A-Thon.

That day, the Gardens had hosted a Jehovah's Witnesses event and all the concessions had been closed because they didn't expect to sell any pop or hot dogs. What the Gardens staff didn't realize was that a majority of the 18,000 people who came to the event brought food in plastic or paper lunch bags and pop in cans. At the end of the event, the building was a complete mess.

Bernie didn't have a clean-up crew because he didn't think he would need one, and the garbage company the Gardens was using, Laidlaw, wouldn't pick up the phones because it was a Friday night. We looked around the place and told them, "Go home. We'll take care of it."

Ted and I scoured the local streets, rounded up some homeless guys, and spent the entire night cleaning up the Gardens. We grabbed bag after bag, can after can, and crammed all the garbage into the back of our K-car and shuttled load after load to the dump. Then we swept the entire facility.

Just as Bernie came in at seven on Saturday morning we finished the mopping and the place was spotless. We were totally spent. Meanwhile, the car was soaking wet and it looked and smelled disgusting. We thanked Bernie for the opportunity and took off to recover.

We got a call from him on Monday. He thanked us, told us we did a good job, and asked for our invoice. Then he invited us to meet Ian Clark, the controller of Maple Leaf Sports and Entertainment. We gladly came in with our invoice and Ian told us how he appreciated what we did, how he thought it was kind of insane, and how he would like to offer us the opportunity to take over Laidlaw's contract.

Of course, we were ecstatic. We agreed to the deal and within a week we were pulling all the recycling and garbage out of Maple Leaf Gardens on a regular basis. We bought a van, then a cube van, and we leveraged the Gardens deal into contract wins with the Royal York and the Delta Chelsea hotels. We then went after some of the larger entertainment and hospitality venues, kind of introducing recycling to them, and our business grew by leaps and bounds.

At this point we moved out of my parents' garage and into a small unit in Markham, Ontario. A year later we rented a bigger unit in Etobicoke, a suburb in Toronto's west end. It was a wild way to start, but that's how we got going.

*   *   *

Before our big break in 1986–87, Ted had gone to university and I worked in the financial industry. In 1990 I noticed that Bell Canada was putting out its invoices on recycled paper, so I developed a recycled paper/stationery line to sell at universities and gift stores. Around this time, Ted went to work at a large industrial real estate broker, where he started noticing the high number of recycling companies that were leasing space.

The two of us had been friends since high school, so we started chatting. Next thing you know we figured out how to combine a recycled-paper business with recycling pickup. We would offer recycled photocopy paper to businesses, and when we delivered the paper we would pick up their scrap at no charge. It was pretty innovative at the time.

In the beginning, we'd go to our jobs during the day and at night we'd work on our business. Things didn't start out well. There were many times when we'd question whether it was worth continuing. Sometimes I think the secret of our success was that we were just too stupid to quit. If anybody had sat down with us and pointed out how, from a practical perspective, we were picking up garbage in a K-car and trying to compete with full-fledged waste management companies, I think we might have seen the light.

But, of course, the great thing about a partnership is that both of you almost never have these doubts at exactly the same time. Through the years this has worked out well for us. When Ted has been a little concerned, I've been there to say, "Don't worry about it," and vice versa.

We were both raised in Canada and are of Greek descent. We come from very loud families, so we have our issues and we get into it, but at the end of the day we definitely see eye-to-eye. The tension is actually pretty good, because it's a competitive tension. Throughout, we constantly focus on what the customer is looking for and on what it's going to take to grow our business. Today Ted predominantly does our commercial sales while I handle our plant operations and municipal and commodity sales. We're both salespeople at heart.

But when we started out we didn't have any capital, and we needed our full-time jobs to survive. The lack of resources was our biggest challenge. At the same time, we always tell people things happened the way they were supposed to happen. Frankly, we probably would have lost the capital if we'd had it in the early days when business was slow.

Some of our other challenges included learning management and administration, including how to deal with staff. Neither of us had spent very long working in an organization, so the hiring and firing of our first employees were pretty traumatic events. We came from blue-collar families, so we understood how important it was for someone to come home with a paycheque. It was tough. And, by the way, it's still not easy today when we make the wrong decision and have to let someone go.

After we got Maple Leaf Gardens and those subsequent big contracts were signed, the popularity of our services soon outstripped our administrative capabilities. As a result, keeping on top of regulations and paperwork, payroll, and all those important tasks became impossible.

We really had to start thinking about how to leverage our time, and how to find the right people to help us operate the business. Not just people with the right skills, but those who would fit our corporate culture. There are a lot of smart people out there who couldn't work in these spartan conditions or work at a company that's growing by 50 per cent to 60 per cent a year; you need to be a little bit off the wall. Getting the right people on board was a huge challenge.

I found that if we can hire fanatical people, people that are passionate about sustainability, that's the one thing our competition cannot deal with. They simply can't compete with a fanatical sales force. That's our goal.

* * *

Currently, Turtle Island has about 450 employees, about $80 million in sales, more than 200 trucks, and 10 facilities—nine in Ontario, with an oil-recycling facility in Edmonton. Over the years we have had many successes, but they have not come without risk and heartache.

For example, in 2005 we decided to bring in people who could help us grow our business, and so we sold 50 per cent of our business to a private equity firm. It wasn't an exit strategy; it was a growth strategy. We were looking for partners with experience in growing businesses.

There were some hiccups, but the private equity firm is still our partner today. They really helped us understand business administration more clearly. It also helped us get better at finding the proper mid-management-type people to help the company grow, which was very important to us.

We have actually risked our business on a couple of occasions as well.

In 2000, we bid on a very large municipal contract in Toronto, and if we had gotten it wrong we could have gone bankrupt. It was a very difficult time for us; not only were we having trucking issues, but it was our first time in the municipal collection business. Right now we're the largest in Ontario, so it's been very successful, but we risked the business to become a municipal operator as opposed to a strictly commercial operator.

One of the most amusing events in the history of our company—the move to our current facility—was also one of the scariest.

In September 1993 the landlord at our old facility in Etobicoke told us he was selling the building and we had to be out by April 30, 1994. It's very difficult to get permits to run recycling facilities and nobody wants to have a recycling facility near their property. We approached a guy named Len Vigoda who owned Fibre Resource Recovery, the predecessor of Sonoco Recycling. Len was leasing an 118,000-square-foot facility at the Port of Toronto. We asked for just 5,000 square feet of the pier he wasn't using. We promised to give him any of the cardboard we collected in our daily pickups—and to pay him rent, of course.

He agreed, saying, "No problem, just move in." Then we heard nothing. By December 1993 I had started calling Len to organize the signing of the lease. No response. January and February went by without a word, even with my multiple daily calls. By March we still had no response. Finally, there we were on April 30, without a lease and homeless. We had to vacate the old place, so we just packed up and moved into the space that Len had promised us.

We were pretty worried. We were trying to be very quiet so no one saw us. Luckily it's a big place, and nobody did. Believe it or not, we just kept on working there without a lease.

Around the end of 1994, Sonoco came in and bought Fibre Resource Recovery, and their management changed. A new guy named Jean-Pierre Poliquin took charge, and still no one paid much attention to us. Now we were using 10,000 square feet, having doubled our requirements over six months as the business grew. Our trucks would go back and forth. We'd always wave to JP as we drove in and he'd wave back. Meanwhile, the landlord to the City of Toronto, Dov Altman, was also someone we'd chat with or wave to when we went past.

One day I was driving in my pickup and both JP and Dov were in the front building area. It was like having two girlfriends, walking into a restaurant, and seeing them both sitting there having coffee. So while I knew this couldn't be good, I waved to both of them and they both waved back—just our standard greeting. Then, unbeknownst to me, they started talking about us. Dov said something to JP like, "You know, it's awfully nice of you to rent space out to those kids. They work awfully hard. I see them early in the morning and they're often here late at night too." JP looked up and said, "I'm not renting any space to those kids. They're your tenants," and Dov, shocked, said, "No, no, no, they're not ours!"

JP immediately cut the power to our building. Not knowing anything serious was amiss, I knocked on his office door and asked if something might be wrong in the electrical room. I remember this clearly. He said, "Either you're the stupidest guy I've ever met in my life or the smartest. I don't know yet."

We hadn't paid rent in almost a year, and the reason was we didn't want to know how much it was going to cost. But we were even more afraid of approaching someone to offer payment, fearing they would kick us out because we didn't have a signed agreement. Without a facility, we'd probably go out of business.

In the end we became really good friends with JP and he became my mentor. We cut him a cheque for the back rent that afternoon and became his sub-tenants. He taught us a lot about the business over the years. Ultimately, as he was winding down his operations at the pier in 1994, he sold them to us. That really, really helped and our business just took off. We were lucky he was an understanding guy.

Of course, another reason we're still here as a company is persistence.

The obvious way to be successful as an entrepreneur is to pick something to do and stick with it. You have to really work hard at it. You have to realize nothing is going to happen overnight. Almost all gains you make are incremental, so you must give yourself time. Don't give yourself six months or you'll fail before you even start. Give yourself 10 years and make sure you're prepared to make the commitment. Then look around you; take a look at your friends and your family, because you're not going to see them for those 10 years. My wife Laura and I have been together 25 years, since we were teenagers. I'm sure I've let her down. I can't remember the kids' first six birthday parties; I missed them all. It takes its toll on families. So marrying right is very important, too.

TED: We gave up everything: high school friends, my university friends, relatives. We just cut ourselves off and put the blinders on. The truth is if you have a lot of other possible careers to fall back on you've probably got too many options. Eliminate all your options. Tell yourself, "This is all I've got. If I haven't got this I'm done." Don't give yourself an out.

I have a friend I visit every so often. He's part of a great family. I love these people, and one reason is they're four generations into a business they run beautifully. No fighting, no sibling rivalry. If that was a Greek family they would have been at each other's throats. Their grandfather started the business many years ago.

At one of their charity functions I saw the members of this family sitting at the tables, and it was the grandkids. The grandfathers were dead, the fathers were dead, and now the grandkids and their kids were still doing business together. I was so impressed. We were sitting down and my billionaire friend said, "I really admire what you and your partner have done with Turtle Island. You guys have done a great job." I said, "You admire me? What the heck are you talking about? What you guys did was ten times harder than what we've done."

My point was that Louis and I had no pressure but we still excelled. The lack of pressure was exactly why I think it was easier for us. Our families are great, middle-class, blue-collar people and they gave us a foundation, but if we had failed it wouldn't have been a disaster. No one said that we had to put food on the table because we were living at home. No one said that we had to raise kids because we weren't married. No one said that we'd better not mess up this business our grandfather started because it's worth $100 million.

In contrast, those guys are damned if they do and damned if they don't. If they lose the business, people will criticize them for their incompetence, and if they make it big everyone will say, "Well, it was your dad's money."

What we did was easy. We did everything on our own; we didn't borrow from anybody. We didn't have any burden on us. We were free to think. We had no mentors—until Jean-Pierre came along. What we learned, we learned from each other, and that's why we trust each other. We didn't have our fathers looking over our shoulders, questioning our every move. We were lucky enough to have free rein and make our own choices.

When I hear some young kid say something like, "I want to get some experience right now, do something fun, because at the end of the day I know I'm going to go work for my dad's company," I lose it. I once heard this sentiment from a young guy. He was university educated, good looking and smart and I told him to his face: "You're being deliberately mediocre, and it's because you've got this family thing to back you up!" Here's a guy with looks and an education from the best universities, and he wants to be mediocre! I think you have to give your children the ability to go out and make mistakes and to learn the hard way. They'll feel better and they'll feel prouder. The last thing you want is to be known as "daddy's kid."

In our case, our parents were always proud of us, but they were very concerned that their kids wanted to pick up garbage for a living. In the first couple of years it looked like they were right. It was just brutal. There was no money and there were sometimes 20-hour workdays. They said, "Give it up. Stop. You guys are smart. Go find jobs someplace. You can't compete with big trucks by running around with a van."

So when we made our first profit, $80,000, we both decided that, for all the grief we'd caused our parents over the last few years, we'd take the money and buy them each a car. Our parents never had nice cars so we bought them each an identical Mercedes. That's where our first profit went. Each car cost $33,000; this was in 1995. They stopped saying those types of things because they knew our hearts were in the right place.

LOUIS: I think the key to success is to always focus on your core competencies and on your customers. When someone cancels our service it's the biggest wake-up call because it's like getting a divorce. If this happens a lot, you've got problems. You have to quickly figure out what went wrong and try to improve. Sometimes it has happened because of a bad driver and sometimes because of a better price. Either way, it probably happened because we forgot about the customer. You really need to be on edge. If you're on edge you'll be okay because you will react swiftly. When people tell us it's not working and they throw us out, we regroup and hit back fast.

Remember, we're in a place where we're allowed to make mistakes. We're in the greatest country in the world. You can get right back up and keep trying again and again. There are some countries where you don't get the chance to set up a bank account. So we're happy to take those risks. Sure, there are times when you have to listen to a person who might say, "Hey, this might not be a smart idea," but when you've been doing something a long time—and we've been doing this for 21 years—sometimes you just know. You can't put it on paper, you can't budget for it, it's just a gut feeling you have about what the customer wants. A lot of it is intuition, and it's hard to budget for. It's also hard to articulate to investors and shareholders, so sometimes the only way you can do it is to act; just show them.

TED: Being an entrepreneur takes hard work and a little bit of luck. People say if you work hard you create your own luck. I don't believe that. There are millions of people who work hard and don't have luck. To me, luck is relationships—meeting the right people and treating them right. And by relationships, I don't mean knowing the presidents of dozens of companies. No, it's about knowing the shoe-shine guy. I can't tell you how many people call me who are cleaners, repairmen, or garbage men, right up to the CEO of a company. So when a guy calls me and says, "My brother-in-law is opening a restaurant, go see him," it's like the president or CEO is calling us. We're going in there with no bid, no competition, and we have a great shot at providing the service. That's something you cannot take for granted and it's something you should try to reciprocate if you can. That's called a relationship.

LOUIS: I think the majority of entrepreneurial businesses fail because people can be very myopic. You might be a great engineer who built something great, but just having something great doesn't mean you're going to be able to sell it.

There are three key ingredients you have to be on top of all the time in order to fly. You need to get the right people, you need to have the right product, and you need good marketing. But if one of those things is accelerating ahead of the others your plane will be a little lopsided, so you had better start working on your service offerings and making sure you have the right people on board to execute them. All three have got to be moving at the same speed. If operationally you're doing fine but your marketing team can't sell the product, then what good is it?

TED: So many entrepreneurs invest without the means. Don't invest capital. The only capital you should invest is your sweat, your human capital. Don't invest money unless you know you can sell the thing. We used to sell first and then figure out how to make a dime on it.

People will sit and study forever, and there's so much information out there that it can hinder your ability to make any decisions. These people become paralyzed. If you go on the Internet, for every argument that says garlic is good for you, there are another 14 pages that say it's bad for you. But there's nothing like being out in front of a customer to really tell you what the pulse is. You want to know how your grocery store is doing? Go out there and sit in the aisles and see what they pick up and what they put back. Or go and speak to customers. If you're starting a business, talk to prospective customers first. What a concept!

It's easy to write cheques and be theoretical, looking at numbers and projections. You know what? Get off your ass and wear out a few pairs of shoes. I've got four pairs of shoes in my car right now and they're all worn out. I'm going to get them resoled. I'm not on my butt behind a desk and neither is Louis.

I think what really drives us, besides the thrill of hiring good people and watching them thrive, is the way our services benefit the environment. We save ten thousand trees a day just through our recycling efforts. We love going into new buildings and showcasing our efforts. We love to take a building—for example, the Hudson's

Bay Head Office at Bay and Queen in Toronto—and completely eliminate their waste. After we did this for The Bay, they got a third-party audit and then invited reporters and TV crews and told their recycling story to the world. And all that just really makes us want to do this even more.

There are so many more ideas that could help save the planet, such as cutting carbon emissions, pollution, and water consumption. There's so much more we can do. We're doing our part, which is a pretty significant part, but in the grand scheme it's very, very small.

LOUIS: The recycling industry is in its salad days. We see ourselves being more involved in making things in the future, being able to turn people's belongings into useful products and so eliminate landfills, which are old and antiquated. We don't need them anymore.

We plan on being a force for many years. Of course, it's not easy to stay on top. In 2008, when the credit markets got crunched, we had millions and millions of dollars of materials being shipped all over the world—scrap, cardboard, metal. A lot of it never reached its destination because letters of credit wouldn't flow. We lost millions. We're semi-insulated because we have a lot of different services, including our recycling services, waste services, plant operations, and transfer stations. If you are somewhat diversified in our industry, with a healthy balance, these downturns can be the greatest thing to happen for your business. The guys that survive pick up the spoils.

It's been tough for us. Still, we are coming out of the downturn a much leaner, meaner company. We were able to react fairly quickly. We have also made some important acquisitions over the past four years.

Clearly the worst thing about challenging economic times is that you can't predict them. Entrepreneurs have to understand that you make it in this business through those small, incremental advances. Businesses are built over long periods of time. This instant success phenomenon people talk about? I haven't seen it.

We talk to young people all the time and they ask us about running a business. We tell them it's extremely important to realize that you're not the boss. You might be steering the ship, but as soon as you start thinking you're the boss it's the end of your business.

Employees are part of your team, but the boss is your customers. You have to be approachable enough that your employees can come in and talk to you—really talk to you—and have difficult discussions and meetings; that's real collaboration. The way I know we've had a good meeting is if people are upset at the end. If that's happened, people have said things not everyone agreed with. That's okay. Surrounding yourself with people who tell you only what you want to hear is a trap. They won't bring you their ideas and you're above everyone. Both Ted and I are surrounded by people at work; we don't have offices and our meetings can get pretty loud. It doesn't matter if you're the guy running the forklift in the plant—when you're in a meeting and you disagree or you've got something important to say, in this place you say it.

A lot of our ideas come from the front lines, which helps make those people feel part of the team. A boss is more of a figurehead than anything else, anyway. Who's at the front lines? Our customer service people, our sales team, our Environmental Department members who go out and talk to businesses about how they can reduce waste. These are the people we need to take care of. Our job is to support them. If we can do that, our customers will be delighted, and if we're delighting our customers there's always more business coming down the road.

12
KNOWING WHAT YOU DON'T KNOW

Even Entrepreneurs Need a Strong Team to Succeed

RIVERS CORBETT

Restaurant franchise chain

"I'm a firm believer in knowing what I don't know."

RIVERS CORBETT

TYPE OF BUSINESS: *Restaurant franchise chain* | FOUNDED: *Fredericton, New Brunswick, 2009*

www.relishme.ca

ENTREPRENEURSHIP ISN'T FOR EVERYONE. If you want to become an entrepreneur you need to be able to deal with adversity. I've certainly had my share.

I have always been an entrepreneur at heart. When I was in my early twenties, I bought a 1-900 number. Back then most of these numbers were being used for somewhat shady operations, but I bought mine so I could resell it to businesses that might want to conduct surveys. I have also owned a commercial meat wholesale business, a nursing home, a marina, and apartment buildings. What I discovered over the years was that I enjoyed building businesses from scratch a lot more than buying and operating them.

Years ago I bought a nursing home, thinking it would generate a steady stream of income and allow me to lead the life I wanted to live—having a bit of freedom and not being committed to a gruelling work schedule. Unfortunately, I made some poor decisions when I appointed the board members, and the people I thought were my friends threw me out of my own business.

I have also had another business called The Chef Group, which I co-founded after reading an article in Profit magazine about a trend involving chefs providing specialized in-home meal preparation services. My business partner—a chef—and I founded the company with just $3,000 in start-up capital and turned it into a million-dollar operation in only four years. But we eventually decided to part ways, and I was left with a weakened company because my partner had been in charge of all operational issues. Despite building a strong business with a steady stream of income, I was once again forced to find a new way to achieve my long-term financial goals.

I bought out my partner's shares in The Chef Group and continued to run the company. But I knew that if I wanted to take the business to the next level I was going to have to find another chef—or start another business from scratch.

If I was going to start up a new business I wanted it to be in the food industry. The funny thing is that I absolutely hate to cook. Fortunately my wife loves it and is very good at it. But I would dread nights when my wife wasn't home and I had to do the cooking myself. (Luckily my kids now know how to make Kraft Dinner. I can't even stand doing something that simple.)

So why does someone who hates cooking want to work in the food industry? I love the business of food. I really enjoyed my experience with The Chef Group and being able to grow it into a million-dollar company. Since I had no culinary talent myself, I needed to find a skilled chef who could help me start another business.

My opportunity arrived in 2009. I was invited to be a guest server at a charity event hosted by the local chapter of the Canadian Culinary Federation, a national association of chefs and cooks. Chef Ray Henry was the president of the chapter and, as luck would have it, he was in a situation similar to mine. Chef Henry had moved from the West Coast to Fredericton to take a job as an executive chef and had recently lost his position.

Both of us, due to circumstances beyond our control, found ourselves in uncertain territory. Chef Henry had lost a job and I was trying to run a food service business without knowing how to cook. We were looking to take the next step in our careers. I saw Chef Henry in action at the charity event and thought he had incredible talent. It was clear he had a great knowledge of food and really knew how to command a kitchen.

Chef Henry and I chatted a bit at the event. Afterwards, I reached out and got a dialogue going between us. Chef Henry didn't want to go back to being a chef at a big establishment. He wanted to do something different where he had more control over his career. I was looking to move on to something different, too. I have never been satisfied with the status quo and wanted to try something innovative in the food industry.

Neither of us knew exactly what to do at first, but I was able to convince Chef Henry to stay in Fredericton for a while until we came up with a plan. The Chef Group was holding cooking classes for Sobeys in their grocery stores and doing some catering, so Chef Henry was able to make some income that way while we figured out our next move.

One day Chef Henry called me and said he had the idea we had been looking for: a gourmet burger operation in Fredericton. At first I thought he was crazy and told him there was no way a gourmet burger store was going to work. But I kept an open mind and we continued talking about the concept. Finally we arrived at an idea we could both agree on. We would make the customer's experience fun and engaging, as much a great experience as the food itself. We thought the idea would set us apart from other establishments and allow us to build the business.

I'm a firm believer in knowing what I don't know. I'm good at putting together the infrastructures to make businesses work. But I didn't have the knowledge of food or restaurants that Chef Henry had. Even though I wasn't completely sold on the gourmet burger idea at first, I put my trust in his ability to recognize what kind of a restaurant experience people would want.

I'm not a big fan of research. I've always thrown caution to the wind. And if the restaurant didn't work out, I figured the start-up costs were relatively low so we wouldn't lose too much money. Eventually I just decided we should give it a try. Our goal was to open the restaurant in December of 2009 and get a boost from the holiday shoppers. Unfortunately we ran into some delays and weren't able to open until January 2010.

Normally opening a restaurant in January isn't great for a business; consumers have spent all their money over the holidays and have little left. So we were worried when we had to open late. But what happened was amazing: we had lineups out the door as soon as we opened.

We decided to call our operation Relish Gourmet Burgers. Most people think it's named primarily for the garnish, but the main meaning for us is the verb. We want to show our customers that we relish them and hope in turn that they will relish their experience at our restaurants.

The key to Relish is to make the experience fun for guests. Making a good burger wasn't going to be enough to set us apart from all the other burger operations in the city. We needed to zag while everyone else was zigging.

The Relish experience begins as soon as someone gets up to the cashier. The cashier asks them for their order, gets their name, and, when the order is ready, our staff will say, "We relish Dave!" or whatever their name happens to be. Sometimes the other customers will even join in. So we have combined a great participatory process with a gourmet burger experience. We want our staff to be enthusiastic, engage our customers, and give them an experience they won't forget.

I always say our goal is to be the Disney World of gourmet burgers. When you think of Disney World, why do people spend money to go there when they could just go to their local fair? It's about the experience, and we want to replicate that at Relish.

That's not to say we don't make exceptional burgers. We do. All our ingredients are fresh, top-quality products. Our beef is 100 per cent certified Angus beef, seasoned with a unique blend of spices. We also offer turkey burgers, which are specially seasoned, as well as a vegetarian patty with a unique mixture of ground button mushrooms and chickpeas.

Our toppings set us apart from the burgers you see at other establishments. For example, our Jersey City burger combines fried field mushrooms, pickled peppers, pancetta bacon, and provolone cheese. Our Greek Tycoon burger has crumbled feta cheese, marinated bell peppers and onions, kalamata olives, and tzatziki sauce. But we haven't forgotten customers who might want something more basic. The Simpleton burger features lettuce, tomato, roasted garlic mayo, and relish. We're also very proud of our gluten-free offerings, which have gotten rave reviews.

Customers who are getting takeout receive their burger in a high-quality paper bag with handles, not the typical, flimsy takeout bag. We want them to feel like they're getting a unique, high-end product and not just a run-of-the-mill hamburger.

Relish isn't just a restaurant—it's a franchise operation. Our plan has always been to build a network of franchises—37 in five years and 101 in 10 years. That's our goal. And we used odd numbers—another example of zagging instead of zigging.

A big part of our early success was due to the buzz we created around the launch. I've been part of the Fredericton community for a long time, and just before our launch I ran into Brad Woodside, Fredericton's mayor —who is a friend of mine—at a "Tweetup," a real-life meeting organized on Twitter. He asked what I was up to and I told him we were setting up a gourmet burger shop.

The mayor got very excited, said he loved burgers, and suggested we name a burger after him. He called up the media and helped us get into the local press. And he even started tweeting, asking his followers what toppings he should have on his burger. He's a very popular mayor and his support really helped get our name into the community and build momentum. We agreed to name a burger after him and called it the Brad Burger.

We're now up to two corporate stores and three franchise locations and we'll be adding Halifax, Nova Scotia, St. John's, Newfoundland, and Antigonish, Nova Scotia in 2012 and more soon. In each location we name one burger after someone from the community, and the burger remains unique to that community. You can't get it at a Relish franchise in another city. So, for example, in Oromocto, New Brunswick, which has an armed forces base nearby, we have The Base Commander. We had the commander of the local Canadian Forces base decide what would go into the burger and after it was created, some of the soldiers drove out to the restaurant in their armoured vehicles—it was great publicity for us.

We've managed to build a very loyal following in a short period of time. It's almost like a cult. On Twitter, one of our followers mentioned that they were buying a $100 gift certificate from Relish and using it as a prize. Someone tweeted back that $100 would buy 2.5 burgers at "that over-priced restaurant." Almost immediately we had 12 people defending us from the person who called us overpriced. They weren't people we knew. They were our loyal customers. The loyalty really overwhelmed me. You don't typically see that kind of support.

Our following goes beyond the areas where we have Relish franchises. I've had people from other cities say they've heard of us, or they've tried us and they wonder when we'll be opening a franchise in their city. That's a real thrill to me. Recently we had Gene Simmons and Shannon Tweed eat in one of our restaurants and they loved it. Shannon said it was the best burger she'd had east of California.

I've been an entrepreneur with various ventures for more than 15 years and I firmly believe the most important aspect of being an entrepreneur is attitude. You really have to be willing to take some risks to get where you want to go. You also need to realize that there isn't instant glory in becoming an entrepreneur. It takes time to get a new business off the ground.

And there will be times when things go wrong and you need to bounce back. You have to believe things will get better and focus on what you need to do to get your business back on track. When things went wrong in my ventures in the past, such as losing my nursing home or my partner in The Chef Group, I would focus on personal development, exercise a lot, and make sure I ate the right kinds of food. It doesn't sound like it has a lot to do with business, but it kept me in a good frame of mind.

*　　*　　*

Putting together a good team is also key to the success of any enterprise. You can't do everything by yourself. I hate cooking and could never have succeeded in the food business without my team.

The team extends beyond the office team. When things get tough—which will happen—you need a good, close team to help get you through those times. I know when things got bad for me I had help from a lot of different people—my family, my friends, my accountant, my pastor.

It really is important to put some thought into assembling the best team for your business. In my case, if I had taken more time to put together the board of directors of the nursing home, I believe I wouldn't have lost it. I really didn't take enough care to protect my interests—and I paid for it.

At Relish, building a great team was important because of our emphasis on customer experience. A lot of our people had little or no culinary skill, but they all had a desire to be part of the Relish team. Our number-one criterion is that each employee must have a willingness and desire to be part of our culture and character, which is really the essence of what we are trying to build. We can teach them the technical skills they need.

Another thing I've learned through the years is that cash is king. You don't necessarily have to have cash in your pocket; you just need to have access to it. I have always been a squirrel when it comes to cash because a rainy day always arrives. If you're not prepared with a positive attitude, a great support team, and access to cash, you'll have a very difficult time surviving those rainy days.

For me, entrepreneurship isn't about making a tonne of money or putting in a ridiculous number of hours. It's about time and freedom. I don't want the business to be too reliant on me because then I'll never have the freedom I'm seeking. My primary goal is for my business to give me a good work–life balance, so I always try to implement systems so that the business can run without me.

Ultimately I'll pass on the day-to-day operations to someone else who can take Relish to the next level. I love to start businesses but I know I don't have the talents required to get the business to the exponential growth stage. When talk turns to managerial expertise, my eyes glaze over.

I know who I am and I know it's inevitable I will want to do something else and build my next shining star. I think anyone who harbours aspirations of being an entrepreneur and starting their own business should feel good about themselves and the contributions they are making to society. Nothing happens in business without entrepreneurs and, as a society, I believe we should be embracing people willing to take the entrepreneurial journey.

13
THE ENTREPRENEUR'S STRUGGLE
Taking the First Step

JORY LAMB
VistaVu Solutions

"Forget dollars—forget all that. As an entrepreneur most of your capital is your vision, time, and energy."

JORY LAMB

TYPE OF BUSINESS: *Software & consulting* | FOUNDED: *Calgary, Alberta, 1996*

www.vistavusolutions.com

I'M SITTING IN AN EMPTY HALL IN THE TINY TOWN OF BASSANO, ALBERTA, hoping someone—anyone—will show up and hear my pitch. I see a little steam rising from the giant urn of coffee I painstakingly brewed and positioned in the back corner of the room. The 40-some folding chairs symmetrically positioned on the parquet floor are making me feel sillier by the minute. Okay, it's my first demo so I didn't have huge expectations, but I did send out 28,000 homemade ads. After a while I'm just clock-watching. It's 9 A.M., 9:15 A.M., now 9:20 A.M. Not a soul enters the hall.

"No problem," I think to myself as I pack up all my clunky computer equipment, throw it in my rented Budget van, and make my way down the Trans-Canada Highway to my next stop in Gleichen, Alberta. "I'm not going to be defeated. I'm going to teach computerless farmers to become technologically savvy if it kills me."

In a hall in Gleichen a guy lets me in and helps me set up. We do it all over again—40 chairs, huge coffee urn, the whole bit. This time it's a lunch-hour talk. Again, nobody comes. The guy who helped me is sitting in the back, so I say, "Since you're here, do you want to see my demo?" He says sure, so I go through the whole show and at the end it's clear he thinks the idea of computerizing the farming business is fascinating. I ask if he would be interested in a solution like this. Not really, he says. He drives a school bus.

I pack up again, throwing everything in the van. Eventually I've gone through a whole day of this and things are really not looking good. As I head home, I'm scratching my head, wondering what the heck is going on. With 28,000 rural mailboxes hit, surely somebody must have been interested.

I'm undeterred. About two weeks later, just as I'm getting ready to get back on the road and do it all again, I get a phone call from a farmer from one of those first towns, and he rips a strip off me. He says they'd have loved to be at my demo but they didn't get the ad until just now. "Get it to me sooner and next time I'll be more than happy to be there," he bellows, though I'm paraphrasing because what he actually said wasn't quite so kind.

That's when I called Canada Post and learned it takes up to six weeks from the time you drop off unaddressed ad mail to the time it gets delivered and placed in the post office boxes. I had only given it a few days.

About $10,000 later, I learned my first entrepreneurial lesson. There is no faster teacher than making a mistake with your own money. I just hoped I could survive to see the end of the curriculum.

*　*　*

My friends and family thought I was nuts. It was 1996, I was 23 years old, and I'd just volunteered to take a $12,000 buyout package from my first job at a great company, Amoco Petroleum, when it restructured. I felt compelled to open up the world of computers, software, and the Internet to Alberta farmers and other small business owners so they could run more efficient operations.

Amoco had treated me very well. I spent about two-and-a-half years performing various accounting functions. I enjoyed my time in Calgary but I found, in the grand scheme of things, that it really didn't matter whether I showed up to work or not. I had no real impact. I always wanted more control over my own fate.

So I rented an office, got business cards printed, installed a phone line, picked a name, put some ads in a local paper, and sat and waited. One of the most sickening emotions I ever felt came while just sitting there, staring at the phone, willing it to ring. Had I made a mistake? I had left this great job, I didn't have a lot of support for my idea, and it was terrifying. People thought I was giving up something pretty good at Amoco, yet here I was in an 8-foot by 10-foot office, praying for the phone to ring. It was pretty lonely.

That's when I decided I would hit the road and offer training, putting together a dog-and-pony show to demonstrate my service offerings. If they could only see what I could do, the orders would start flooding in! I still have it, my 8.5-inch-by-11-inch promotional flyer, filled with promises. I had peppered 28,000 post office boxes from Rocky Mountain House to the U.S. border.

I called my company Canadian Rural Computer Services (CRCS). The idea for it came from an entrepreneurship class I took at the University of Saskatchewan. We were asked to write a business plan and mine was about driving information out electronically to various rural areas in Saskatchewan, how we would deliver it, who would use it, and, of course, what type of information it would be.

I had no industry experience and I didn't grow up on a farm. I grew up on 46th Street in Lloydminster, Alberta. I knew I wanted to do something with IT and systems but it wasn't my background. I had no computer training, I'd never managed a company or staff, and I didn't have any customers or contacts. Knowing what I know now, this was not a good investment.

But I always knew I wanted to be a small business owner. The $12,000 from Amoco represented an opportunity to start something of my own. It also gave me the chance to realize another dream.

I grew up in a large extended family. I'm an only child, but there were 22 cousins, and the majority of us lived within blocks of each other. Easters, Christmases, Thanksgivings, and other occasions were important and included get-togethers and big family meals. They were very special. I always hoped to have the opportunity, when I started my own family, to be the type of dad who was always there to host these events and always physically available to go to those soccer games or ballet lessons. One way to get there would be to achieve financial independence, and the best way to do that was to start my own business.

When the flyer finally hit, people did show up at the demos and training sessions. We partnered with Alberta Agriculture and delivered Internet access and expertise, which in 1996 was lightning in a bottle. The World Wide Web was brand new, and in those days it was Netscape 2.0, Eudora Mail, and AltaVista searches. I provided instruction on farm accounting software and we were even selling computer systems. The business started to get some legs.

Looking back, there's no end of lessons I've taken away. You might ask, "Would I do it again?" What I do know now is that a tremendous amount of energy was expended to make up for my lack of knowledge. If I had the opportunity to do it again, I would absolutely be more knowledgeable about my market and my craft. It wasn't possible in 1996 because time didn't allow me to gain expertise and my impatience didn't allow me to wait. I just pushed on.

In time, CRCS developed three different revenue streams, and for the first three or four years we just threw everything at the wall; if it stuck, that's what we sold. The first revenue stream came from training: Internet use, computer systems, accounting, and things like that. The second area was web development. It was a natural progression in 1996 and 1997 for us to start building all sorts of different websites, and we produced some pretty cutting-edge work for the time. We were pushing the limits of what had been and could be done and applying it to agriculture. For the third area, we built software for the feedlot industry and managed all of the applications.

The web side became a new company of which I'm still a partner now, Core Creative. It looks, acts, and services customers very differently than it did back in 1997. It has its own management and runs on its own. It's a great business and it energizes me to no end when I work with those guys and hear about all the cool stuff they're doing.

The arm that focused on feedlot software became its own company, Feedlot Solutions. The software was written in 1997 and was actually our first product. Through extensive marketing we had landed a contract with a veterinarian who consulted to the feedlot industry, and then we built an application for it.

We even had an application around health safety and food traceability. It was designed so you could locate—if a cow had BSE (mad cow disease), for example—all the other cattle in the feedlot that had come in contact with it. But our client base consisted of about 40 customers in Canada and that was probably as many as we were going to get.

That was when we took our first foray into the United States; in 2002 we just decided to go for it. We went down and set up shop, and it was a veterinarian, Dr. Tom Edwards, in a place called Kearney, Nebraska, who found us on the web. He brought us down and introduced us to some of his clients. We picked up a few there. In time the word started getting out about us. It was just mad marketing, guerilla marketing. We started picking up more and more clients.

Several of these clients migrated from an old DOS program called Dalex to us. Dalex was an American company. Incredibly enough, even though it was headquartered in Minnesota, Galen Loseke, the general manager of Dalex, lived in Kearney, about a mile up the road from Dr. Edwards. They actually went to church together and were old friends. Through this grapevine the general manager of Dalex approached us to begin selling Feedlot Solutions. We agreed, and this became a major tipping point for our penetration into the market.

We didn't actively go after Dalex customers—in fact we kind of did the opposite—but Galen knew so many people and so much about the industry that I put him in charge of Feedlot Solutions. By this time it was its own legal entity; he had built his own team, got it organized, and got rolling. I took care of strategy, new product development, market penetration, marketing, and anything around financial management. He took care of the sales, day-to-day operations, specifications on the new products, and technical support.

The net result was that we entered the U.S. market with 40 clients, and by the time we sold in 2007 we had more than 200. It was a great experience, because it taught me what it's like to do business there. It taught me how to build and grow a company when none of your staff is in the same location as you. I also learned how to sell a company. We decided in 2006 to sell because I was so busy with web-related work and software projects, writing a lot of one-off solutions for customers for Core Creative.

*　　*　　*

But back in Canada we had realized that our business model was fundamentally flawed. We were writing good web and software applications. We also built web interfaces and a customer relationship management (CRM) system that bolted onto another accounting system. But we weren't providing any core solutions for our customers. Nothing we provided ran anyone's day-to-day business. As a result, it was easy to write us in and out of the budget.

Our customers were in agriculture/food as well as oil and gas, and we had a good contract, which we still have, with Alberta Health doing recruitment software solutions for them.

So we asked major companies in three industries, specifically agriculture and oil and gas, "What is the solution you use to run your businesses?" Whether it was Agrium or Syngenta, Monsanto, Exxon, or Petro Canada, they all said SAP.

We decided that whatever we provided as our core system would talk to—or interface with—SAP. We went to SAP and told them we worked with small and medium-sized business enterprises (SMBs). Our timing was fabulous. They had just launched a new enterprise resource planning (ERP) product called Business One that was geared to SMBs.

We courted SAP for about six months before they gave us the green light to become one of the first providers of Business One in Western Canada. We had never implemented an ERP solution in our lives.

We decided the best fit for us was oilfield services. We could take some of our programming expertise, marry it with the capabilities of the product, add extra value through our software add-ons, and sell to a market with an ability and willingness to buy.

Our product, FieldVu, lets oil and gas companies centralize their operations, sales, assets, HR, purchasing, and financial data in a single system. Data about job and unit costing, preventative maintenance, field ticketing, work orders, scheduling, service/repair, inventory, and equipment tracking are captured in the same system. The

ERP system is designed to improve productivity, reduce costs, anticipate challenges, and allow companies to seize new opportunities quickly.

We started selling SAP in 2004 and have had an incredibly successful relationship with SAP ever since. As a result, in 2006 we decided to change the name to VistaVu Solutions—as Canadian Rural Computer Services wouldn't sell in corporate America—and try the U.S. market.

It was time to get schooled again.

We started in Denver because I knew it well from my agriculture background. Even though I understood that Houston was the oil mecca of the United States, I felt more comfortable in Denver. That was a big mistake. We spent a lot of money creating awareness, getting an office, and hiring employees in Denver, but we always got pointed back to Houston. They'd say, "It's a great product but we can't make a buying decision; it has to be made by head office." We lost money, time, and energy in that decision. Realizing my error, we shut down Denver and quickly built a presence in Houston.

I really had more to learn about doing business in the United States. More importantly, I had to learn about hiring. It was hard. With Feedlot Solutions, getting on solid footing in the United States was quick. We were invited down and we largely sold through word of mouth. Things were different in the Houston market. When we went into Houston we knew no one, so it was all headhunters and sites like Monster.com. We struggled to gain traction. Most of the implementations and most of the tech support were delivered from Canada, because we already had a good team here. Through trial and error I learned about the enormous challenge of setting up in a locale where you don't know anyone.

I also learned that part of the reason entrepreneurs make mistakes is a lack of guidance. One of my problems was that I didn't know it was okay to ask for help, to not know the answer to a question, and that it was okay to accept other people's ideas and opinions. In my youth, I perceived all of these actions as signs of weakness.

As a 23-year-old who sometimes wondered why he wasn't running Amoco after two-and-a-half years, I had a level of expectations that didn't leave me open to suggestions, coaching, or mentoring.

Entrepreneurs are beholden to no one, and that's a problem. When I thought we should expand into Denver, people around me might have been thinking it was a bad idea, but either I wasn't willing to hear them or they were not willing to speak up. Someone outside the organization with a track record of business success can speak up and, in a healthy way, challenge you to take the sober second thought often needed to make good decisions, especially strategic decisions.

I did get a great mentor, a guy by the name of Kim McConnell, who is one of the founders and formerly the CEO of AdFarm, an advertising agency focusing mainly on agriculture. During Kim's tenure, AdFarm was recognized three years in a row as one of the top 50 best-managed companies in Canada. This is a quality guy who took me under his wing in 2000 and gave me direction so I could develop a vision. Rather than throwing it all at the wall and seeing what stuck, he set me on a path and gave me the tools and knowledge to execute with a strategic direction in mind.

But we entrepreneurs always want to be right. Still, even while dealing with my type of personality, Kim was great. Sometimes he would tell me things I would just understand instantly. Other times it would be a year later and I'd think, "Ah, now I get it." He helped me become a better business leader.

He also helped me get into the Entrepreneurs' Organization, which has led me to build a better business on a financial level to get me closer to my initial vision: when I have my family, I want to be there. I want to be able to go to the school play or on a ski vacation and not have to say "Sorry, I have to be at work," or "No, we can't afford it."

*　　*　　*

Before Kim came along and before we had a few other important experiences under our belt, I would say that from November 1996 to 1999 we really floundered. We were trying to find our staff and figure out what we offered and how to offer it. An awful lot of unnecessary energy was expended.

I think everybody has only so much life in their battery—their energy level. Everybody's is different, but if you deplete it chasing things that aren't getting you where you want to go, you can only recharge that battery so many times before it won't go back up to full. Kim helped me understand my return on energy. Forget dollars—forget all that. As an entrepreneur most of your capital is your vision, time, and energy.

And it comes full circle. For me, the single greatest thing I did was to call on outside expertise. The moment I accepted I didn't have to know all the answers, that it was okay (although scary), to not know, things started getting easier. I learned to listen.

The juice for me is setting up the business and watching it thrive, as when I gave Brad Peterson, the managing partner of Core Creative, an opportunity to take charge, then provided him with the resources and experience to aid in his success. I believe the best learning comes from some of life's struggles and I've been running a small business since I was 23. I'm 38 now. I have accumulated a war chest of lessons learned and I continue to learn daily.

I'm a part of the Entrepreneurs' Organization (EO) for this reason. I'm a great fan of the entrepreneurial spirit. We have a program called Accelerator for budding entrepreneurs who are trying to break $1 million in sales. It's a global EO program, but Calgary has a chapter of EO members. In July of 2010 I went to the board of EO Calgary and presented a business case to set up an Accelerator program in the city. Since then we have 21 companies and counting. In 2011, I was asked to head up all the global Accelerator programs outside the United States.

It's incredibly rewarding. The energy these people bring to their businesses, and what they're learning, is phenomenal. As I look outward, I want to help more ambitious people become entrepreneurs and take ownership of their own fate. I want to help them avoid some of those expensive lessons I've already lived through.

*　　*　　*

I'm at peace today with my mistakes. I'm a competitive guy. I like to win, and I like the thought that if I mess up and it doesn't work out, it's okay as long as I leave with a useful lesson. And when things do go well, I always relish the experience. I don't necessarily relish the cash or the accomplishment—it's the experience. For example, I still smile when I think about the people at Feedlot Solutions, what a great team they were, and how much fun I had working with them.

So if people have the desire, being an entrepreneur is a most rewarding way to exist. Every day, entrepreneurs raise everyone's standard of living. John D. Rockefeller, Henry Ford, Bill Gates, and Thomas Edison are just a few examples of entrepreneurs who have created employment and economic wealth while contributing to the advancement of society. It's definitely a lifestyle and not a career. We're a unique breed. Just ask the spouse of any entrepreneur; we're everything all wrapped into one. We're bipolar, we're ADD. When things are good they've never been better, and when things are bad, they could never get worse. But I've enjoyed the experience and, long-term, it's been very good to me and my family.

The most important advice I could give another entrepreneur is to take the first step. I set out to revolutionize the family farm and today we are one of the top SAP business partners in North America servicing the oil and gas industry. I also have co-owned other businesses, helped would-be entrepreneurs get started and grow, gained financial freedom, have a beautiful family, and am able to live my passion daily. All of this has come as a result of taking that first step.

None of this was part of the plan when I hung the shingle and said, "Okay, CRCS is open for business, please call." Where you start is not necessarily where you end up. It's all about the experience. It's fun and it's stressful.

I still have the same amount of enthusiasm today. I may even have more, but it comes from a different place. Early on I had a lot of trepidation and fear that I don't necessarily have today. I can see where I want to go and how I want to get there. Before, my enthusiasm grew when I made a sale. It was, "Yes! Now we've got another customer—we're growing!" Today my enthusiasm comes from helping someone else get there and seeing if I can play a small role in their success.

Sometimes people see me as a risk taker, because I am an entrepreneur. Actually, I'm a very conservative businessman. Sure, I take risks, but they are usually highly calculated. There's always an understanding of the limit or the downside. Everything has been dissected six ways to Sunday.

I'm responsible for the livelihoods of about 30 people at my organization so I believe they deserve to go to bed at night thinking I'll be conservative in the risks I'm taking. They should have the confidence to know that tomorrow, when they come to work, the lights will still be on.

But I didn't always know where we were headed, and sometimes I had to take risks. There were times when we were technically insolvent. However, a great turning point for me as a leader was about to come.

This was the most critical time during my years in business. It was during the early period, 1999–2000, when all my troubles collided. I was scared to sell—just nervous about having to pick up the phone. Once I was in the sale I was better, but getting there was a real effort. I managed to eventually bleed the cash out of the company. I was tired, mentally defeated. I was just worn out because I had done so much heavy lifting to stay afloat. I had to get out.

I actually took a trip. I went away for six weeks, which is a huge amount of time for someone with a company that is technically insolvent. My family loaned me enough money to cover the bills for six weeks. It was love money. I took this money and I said to the people working for me, "You work with our creditors and make sure that the payments get made. These are the dates. Please, just make sure it happens."

I went to Australia, where I had a lot of "windshield time." I took buses, backpacked, and just kind of followed the countryside. And I read like a madman, searching for an answer to my many questions. One of the books I read was *The E-Myth* by Michael Gerber, which asked whether you planned to work in your business or on your business.

I remember I was in Townsville and there was this huge cyclone. It washed out the road and the bus was stuck. We couldn't go back or forward, and I had nothing but time on this bus. I remember thinking right at this point, "If it's going to be, it's up to me." I had to decide I was not ready to quit. I needed to pull myself back up and make this thing work. I needed to listen. I needed to learn. At that moment, everything changed. A light went on.

Maybe it's kismet, but it was shortly after this that I connected with my first mentor, Kim McConnell, and soon after that we started landing some really good contracts. I had a new mindset; I had made the decision to succeed. We got through it, but it was an experience I will remember for a long time.

I wrote out a plan, communicated it, and got focused. As a business, we were building a bit of everything, always scrambling. What we needed to do was build a few things well. We shed work we were doing just a bit of but weren't good at, and all of a sudden it started to make a huge difference. Part of that planning process came with help from EO and part of it was me recognizing the problems and understanding that we needed to change them.

But I had to stand on the precipice. If we hadn't faced bankruptcy I think somehow, some way, I would have rationalized bobbing along, not really making a good living, not really performing well as a company. Somehow that would have continued to be acceptable and I wouldn't have had to go out and sell and do the things I wasn't enjoying as much. But there was no choice. It was a great thing.

Another great thing happened on March 2, 2010, when my wife and I had a baby girl, our first. It was the realization of another dream. I have spent more time away from the office with my family than ever before and I am loving every minute of it. When I was 23, I didn't know if, when, or how I would have a family, I just knew that I would. I didn't know how I would be available or what my financial situation would be, but I wanted to be in a position to take care of my family and be there for them. I don't want to overstate it, to say that everything is perfect, but I am living it. I've gained the chance to realize what I set out to do, though there is always room for more.

On June 28, 2011, we added our second little girl to the Lamb family. We're on a roll. They are 16 months apart and doing great.

It really has been a rewarding year. VistaVu Solutions won the Better Business Bureau Ethics Award for 2011. I am particularly proud of this award because it validates us a company of the highest integrity. Also in 2011, I was named one of Calgary's Top 40 Under 40 by *Avenue Magazine*.

I don't worry about missing work when I am with my family. The way I look at it, this is my latest challenge—to build up this business so it doesn't need me. In doing so, I can pursue my two passions in life—my family, and helping other would-be entrepreneurs to just take that first step.

14

THE BUSINESS OF MENTORING LEADERS

Bringing It All Home

NATALIE MACAULAY

Partner and UK Managing Director, Emerge Learning

"Don't worry about steps two, three, and four.
If you only know the first step, concentrate on it.
It's called incremental learning, and I'm a firm believer."

NATALIE MACAULAY

TYPE OF BUSINESS: *Leadership development & employee training* | FOUNDED: *Calgary, Alberta, 2006*

www.emergelearning.ca

AS SOMEONE WHO TAKES GREAT EFFORT TO AVOID, even buck, preconceived notions, it's surprising to think that one of my most memorable life-changing moments would be the day I finally knew what it felt like to be a round peg in a round hole.

Up until then, my entire career in Canada (I was born in the UK) had been with large blue-chip organizations. And, to be honest, despite my many successes as a corporate human resources generalist, I always felt like a round peg in a square hole. Then I set foot inside the consulting world of Emerge Learning, which specializes in leadership development and employee training, and for some inexplicable reason I immediately knew I had found what I was supposed to do in life.

If you've never had the experience it might not make sense to you, but it was like finding my calling. It came easily to me; I was successful, it was paying the bills, and I knew I could never go back to working inside a large organization.

I was made to be a consultant and, luckily for me, discovered it before it was too late.

It was 2007 and my new-found passion for learning and consulting was propelling me forward. After a short time as a consultant with Emerge Learning, I was approached to become a partner with the intent of some day assuming a management role. Then, in 2008, I returned to the UK for personal reasons—throwing a spanner into the works, or so I thought at the time.

With the blessing of Emerge Learning, I returned home to be near my family. I was enjoying my consulting role so much that I decided to set up a small business over there under my own title, borrowing the Emerge "blueprint."

There's an organization in the UK called Business Link that helps small businesses get off the ground. Of course I was interested in any help I could get, so I signed up for one of its services, an early start business review. I remember the representative sitting in my home. The country was already heading into a recession, and she was quite forthright that I should not expect much success.

I suppose she was being pragmatic but she kept pushing me on my financial targets and, before I knew it, I was annoyed. I felt patronized, like she didn't really believe in my business, and finally she just pushed me too far.

Plucking a number out of thin air, I told her my new consulting business, Pelorus Learning, would do £150,000 in the first year. She looked at me as if to say, "Are you on drugs?"

The moral of the story is she didn't know me. She was simply acting on what she knew of the environment. I, on the other hand, had been given a challenge. Don't try to tell me I can't do something because I will come back at you in spades. I'm happy to report that not only did I meet Pelorus Learning's initial target, I exceeded it by 33 per cent. And if I truly were malicious, I'd hunt her down myself to tell her so.

Almost a year to the day of my return to the UK, I received a call from Emerge Learning's managing partner, Lee MacLean. She was coming to Europe for a vacation and wanted to see me. I can still hear her first words when we met: "Okay. Stop fluffing around over here and get back into the Emerge family. We want you back in the company, we want you as a partner and we still want you to take over the business some day." This was beyond my wildest expectations.

To be offered the opportunity a second time, when I thought I had turned my back on it to put my family first, was a defining moment in my career. One year later, on June 1, 2010, we sat in the lawyer's office and signed all the papers. I officially became a partner in Emerge Learning Corp. and Emerge took 100 per cent ownership of Pelorus Learning, my UK business.

People are often amazed by my Pelorus story for a couple of reasons. Not only did I start my company at the height of a world economic crisis, but revenue exceeded $350,000 in its first year. When I'm asked about my success, I attribute it to three things. First and foremost is a very large dose of luck. I just seemed to be in the right place at the right time. Then there's my network of contacts which, as an entrepreneur, I consider to be my lifeline. I was able to engage clients straight away in the UK by leveraging my network. And number three, to be quite honest, is hard work. There's no question I had to put the effort in, which meant a lot of travel and a lot of late nights. I'm so grateful to have had the support of my family. When I returned to the UK in 2008, I was homeless, without a job, and starting a new business. Having family support was incredibly important to me.

Perhaps my biggest business challenge at the time was overcoming the sheer panic that set in when I realized I was starting from scratch. From administration to marketing to information technology, to going out and meeting with clients, I had this overwhelming sense of where do I start?

While trying to launch my business, I was also setting up a home and organizing my life. It would have been very easy for me to be disheartened early on, because I experienced my share of setbacks. I couldn't find anywhere to live, I had one project with a client cancelled, and my relationship ended all at the same time.

Fortunately, I think things happen for a reason. To get through that period, I relied on one of my mantras: Don't worry about steps two, three, and four. If you only know the first step, concentrate on it. It's called incremental learning, and I'm a firm believer.

This was validated after I had my first helicopter lesson. The very first day I sat in the cockpit of a helicopter, I realized how important it is to take things step by step. Both legs had to control pedals, my left arm was responsible for one thing and my right arm for another, and all the while I was listening to a radio, knowing I've got this huge, unpredictable machine underneath me.

For me, flying lessons are a fabulous reminder of what I am trying to do in business. I'm helping people learn in incremental steps, because sometimes they can feel as if they're being pulled in a thousand different directions and haven't got a clue what to do next.

*　*　*

Many of my clients are business leaders and, let's face it, leaders have a tough life. Anything a leader does is magnified by an order of 10, 100, or more. You're having a bad day? Too bad, you're the leader. There are problems? They're always going to fall on the shoulders of the leader.

Sometimes I'm asked to work with leaders who may not think they're part of the problem. They know enough to engage the services of Emerge Learning but they think the team is the problem. I find ways of helping those leaders realize they're not only a part of the problem; they need to be part of the solution.

Ultimately, in my business, I'm really just trying to get people to work better together. One of the questions I always revert back to is this: Will somebody die if we don't do this? There are very few times you can answer "yes" to the question. Sometimes it's the only question needed to get a dysfunctional team back on track after things have been blown way out of proportion. It's at those times that I rely on my military training to keep me grounded and to remind me that sometimes we take things too seriously in business.

From an early age, I dreamt of becoming a naval officer. When I was told at age 15 that I didn't have what it takes, I felt the first trigger of indignation inside of me. My reaction was, "Oh yeah? Well, let me show you." Not only did I pass the Admiralty Interview Board two years later, I was offered a bursary to the Britannia Royal Naval College in Dartmouth, Devon, where I was awarded the Queen's Binoculars as most outstanding cadet. You might say I don't take "no" for an answer; it's more like a challenge being issued.

My military training taught me what it was like to work in a male-dominated environment and how to be resilient without sacrificing my femininity. I think a lot of women in business fall into the trap of trying to be more like men. For me, it's been about learning to assert myself and demonstrate from the start that I don't necessarily match the preconceived notions people hold of me. I often refer to it as "upside-down thinking." After reading my bio, people expect to see a tough, hardened, former naval officer. I enter the room with a gentle smile on my face and try to share a laugh or two.

The number-one ingredient to my success in business is my ability to laugh at myself. It's a characteristic I carry over from my years in the military. The navy is an incredibly tough environment, and if you take it all to heart you won't survive.

I like to think I'm a fairly happy-go-lucky person and I find humour is a great way to connect with people. It can be very disarming, but in a positive way. You've got to be able to laugh at yourself and fortunately, or unfortunately as the case may be, I tend to give myself lots of material to work with. It's what gives me the confidence to walk into a room full of tough operations managers. After all, having worked on a warship, I should be able to sit down and talk with them easily.

*   *   *

There's a difference between leadership and management. Often, leaders move up through the ranks, through what Emerge Learning calls individual contributor roles. They become experts in something and suddenly they find themselves at the helm as leader. One of the first steps they must take to become an engaging leader is to get rid of the notion that they're supposed to know all the answers. In fact, they need to accept they will never have all of the answers. From there it's about personal growth and helping leaders to be comfortable in their own skin, because you can't lead a team if you have insecurities about your own performance.

One reason for our success at Emerge Learning is that we live and breathe our own advice every day. We absolutely had to practise what we preach about leadership to get through the recession. We had to tighten our belts and continually seek out opportunities to make things better. We spent a lot of time revamping our processes—consulting for ourselves, you might say.

There's something quite magical about the Emerge brand. Yes, we've got great people, but so do other companies. We have processes, but so do others. What sets us apart is that when we engage clients, we feel we're doing it to have fun and to help people. Of course we need money, but money is an enabler, just like our technology.

As a consulting company, all we have to sell is our ideas, and there are always people out there who are simply looking for free advice. Some of our competitors are very forceful about not giving their expertise away, and they protect themselves by wanting to see the money before engaging a client. At Emerge Learning we're confident enough to believe if we give the business advice freely then companies will feel a connection with us. Then, if they're genuinely interested in the help, why wouldn't they engage us? I can tell you we've only ever fired two clients. In both cases it was because the clients' values simply didn't match our own. One client treated some of our people very poorly. We asked a simple question: Regardless of the profit, does this feel right? The answer was no. The majority of our relationships, I am pleased to say, are long-standing.

This notion of being comfortable in one's skin is perhaps the one that sticks out most when I think of the incredible journey I'm on. It started with my "Aha!" moment the day I walked into Emerge Learning and saw how I fit in. As a round peg in a round hole, I've achieved far more than I ever expected.

Since returning as partner, I find myself in an amazing space between two worlds, with homes in both Canada and the UK. I live a rather strange dual life—where it helps to carry two passports and to know your time zones at all times—but it's actually worked out beautifully. When I wake up in Canada, the first thing I do is tune in to the BBC. Then, when I'm in the UK, I tend to pick up the CBC. I'm always in this sort of dual state.

Yet, no matter what side of the ocean I happen to be on, I couldn't be more comfortable. And I guess that says it all, doesn't it?

15

IN IT FOR THE LONG HAUL

Taming Supply Chain Complexity

KEVIN WONG

Co-founder, Nulogy Corporation

"You should never, ever assume you understand a customer's challenges better than they do."

KEVIN WONG

TYPE OF BUSINESS: *Supply chain software vendor* | FOUNDED: *Toronto, Ontario, 2002*

www.nulogy.com

TODAY NULOGY'S ENTERPRISE SOFTWARE HELPS CONTRACT PACKAGERS, contract manufacturers, and consumer packaged goods companies manage, plan, and operate their production. I know that's a mouthful. To put what we do in simpler terms, I must first describe the industry need we discovered eight years ago.

We actually noticed a number of trends in consumer behaviour that had started to affect big companies like Procter & Gamble and Unilever and the way they were marketing their products and driving sales. Many of these trends can be traced back to an evolution in the area of consumer choice.

For example, instead of buying single ketchup bottles, many of today's consumers go to Costco and buy two ketchups, two relishes, and two mustards as part of a picnic pack because it saves money. Bulk stores are also driving new product formats. Retailers such as Walmart want products at their store to be slightly different from everybody else's so they create exclusive offers—so the consumer can't price compare. Then there are all sorts of "one-off" and repeated promotions—such as when Coke sold soccer-ball-shaped bottles during the 2010 World Cup—that run once, every year, or every few years but just for a limited time.

Also, there is growth in a strategy called "shopper marketing." This is different from consumer marketing. Rather than buying a Super Bowl ad or putting up a giant billboard to get people to buy Dove, for example, consumer goods companies use displays to attract the attention of shoppers in stores. They might offer end-of-aisle displays, clip strips, or little cardboard stand-up displays in the grocery store to catch your eye as you push your cart down the aisle.

These trends have one thing in common: they necessitate product customization before it reaches the retailer. So our clients range from owner-operators to multi-site co-packers, corrugators, and large third-party logistics providers (3PLs). These companies require a high-speed, tightly controlled product or packaging line to make their chocolate bars, apple juice, or personal care products—and it must be customizable for small-format or promotional displays for specific retailers.

Until our solution came along, existing software didn't handle this part of the supply chain well. These activities, in the "last mile" before delivery to the retailer, were very manual and changed extremely rapidly, and there was no consistency in the way things were done. Also, these are largely outsourced activities so people who do them must bid on the work; they're actually selling labour, and they need to watch their margins in real time because job runs are so short. These dynamics, among others, made this extremely challenging.

Users managed such processes on spreadsheets or tried to make do with a generic software system. But such solutions didn't let these firms grow. Spreadsheets are unwieldy. They don't let users open multiple sites and run them all at once. Generic systems are rigid since they aren't built for the task at hand. It's extremely tough to use a system not designed for the way your business works.

When we discovered this gap in the capabilities of the consumer goods industry we were blown away by the possibilities. And by "we," I mean Nulogy's founders. I had gone to the University of Waterloo to study systems design engineering, and there I met several other students who, like me, were budding entrepreneurs. We planned to build a company together.

Still, I had worked at a few places in the U.S., including Ericsson and Microsoft. It was actually pre-Facebook, at a time when Google existed, but was very small, and Apple was kind of still in the doldrums. So Microsoft was very much *the* place to be if you were in technology.

I went there to work with the best and the brightest. And it was great. After a while I realized my co-workers weren't really so incredible, that they weren't really any better than my classmates from university—and that was, in many ways, the impetus for my wanting to start a company.

Also, I figured I'd be better off working on something I helped to create, so I could gain the sort of control I couldn't have working for an organization as large as Microsoft. I enjoyed making big decisions, and ultimately found out I had a talent for it.

Anyway, we decided—along with an engineering professor who is the father of one of the founders—that our business would be one that we could bootstrap. In other words, we wouldn't need initial financing. We studied the Michael Dells and the Bill Gateses of the world and other incredible success stories. Dell and Gates actually dropped out of university to become entrepreneurs, though, and we weren't ready to go down the same path!

We knew we had to stay small. We lived the college lifestyle. We worked on our university computers and together in each other's living rooms. When we had revenue, we moved into an office. But we didn't have much at the start. We were also founding Nulogy at the tail end of the tech bubble bursting. It was risky to start any company at this time, never mind a technology company.

We wanted to prove ourselves by developing a product that served a useful purpose, not by selling vapourware or becoming a dot-com. We had no shortage of ideas. Part of our program years ago had included a design project that we considered our kick at the can for developing a business. While I was interested in the new media space, the plan that had the most legs as a business concept was related to (Jason's father) Dr. Tham's Ph.D. We decided to capitalize on the unfulfilled needs of the consumer goods industry and productize the costing of their highly complex production processes.

Today our data collection and analysis product PackManager is a web-based software that helps part of the supply chain—the contract packagers—by better tracking their inventory, production, and labour information. This tracking is done in real time, so time-saving and money-saving adjustments can be made very quickly. Pack-Shop is a solution for consumer goods companies to more quickly and flexibly develop and execute marketing programs along with a network of suppliers and collaborators. PackShop really helps the consumer goods companies while still depending upon suppliers to use PackManager for the execution of new programs.

When we developed our first product idea we worked with Kellogg's on the proof of concept. And, when we got good feedback, we spent three years protecting our intellectual property, developing our idea, and learning how it could be produced for a particular market.

We sold our first product to a huge, privately owned consumer foods company. Though it took a long time to complete the deal, it was an incredible win. Because we had expertise in costing, the company then asked us to solve another problem in their supply chain related to costing in their contract packaging application.

This new challenge mirrored some research we were engaged in and, as history would play out, this was also a productizable solution. There was huge demand for it. No one had solved this problem, and it would be easy for us to package the software and resell it without too much custom work. We wanted to build something that offered economies of scale—that we could build once and resell 30 times.

Because we built our software to solve existing problems, we listened very closely to our customers—we still do—to determine their needs. Then we built solutions to meet those challenges.

This is very different from what a lot of other firms do. They'll become enamoured of some technology or idea, build it, and then start looking for a customer market. Or they might have a great idea and they go shopping for people to join their company so they can commercialize it.

Luckily, our first customer was one of the largest private consumer foods companies in the world, and when the company rolled out our product, it was the start of many subsequent customer wins.

*   *   *

Another feat we are particularly proud of as a company is the highly effective working relationship we have preserved here over the past eight years. A lot of other firms don't make it that far, let alone with their original founders. Spending so much time together in the early days meant that some very important conversations could take place. We agreed on the company's goals, on who suited which executive roles, what we didn't want to do or become, and so on.

In the end, Jason Tham (CEO) and I (COO) took on the business side of things. I focus on the marketing/product side and Jason focuses on outward-facing/sales activities. Jason Yuen (CTO) manages the engineering team closely, while Sean Kirby (Chief Architect) is the ultimate technical resource and mastermind.

Of course there were speed bumps. As we were building our products, one of our customers lost its contract with its consumer goods company and could no longer use our software. This customer was helping to fund the development of our new solution, so that was a major setback.

Also, our software is complex and very large, and it takes a long time to build. Sometimes development cycle times get extended just when you think you've made a breakthrough. When you're an entrepreneur, it's natural to have nightmares about your problems and to start believing they may never end.

Experts often talk about runways in reference to entrepreneurship and specifically how much money you require before you are forced to take off. For us it was like time spent in a desert. Sometimes it was very tough to believe success was near because the oasis kept coming into view and promptly disappearing again. There's always another challenge. Things never work out entirely as planned.

We were young, and young people weren't typically selling this kind of software to these potential buyers. Plus, it's less common to start a company that sells to an enterprise market. If you're making a product directly for consumers, no one really cares how old you are. Enterprise customers are more established companies and they are quite a bit more risk averse. We didn't have the particular industry experience some thought we should have. We really had to prove our ability to learn the business and solve problems.

On the flipside, we represented fresh blood, set to be injected into an industry typically not perceived to be at the forefront of technology. That was a reason to buy from us, and that was the way we approached things—from a different perspective than other companies.

*　　*　　*

A lot of people ask me how we stay so customer-focused today, even though we're much busier.

It's not easy and it takes time. For instance, customers are more than willing to give you feedback about your product; you just have to give them your ear and be egoless enough to understand they're giving you good insights. You should never, ever assume you understand a customer's challenges better than they do.

But, if you have very few customers—or even just one—you'll be under a huge amount of pressure to react to and/or build whatever they ask for. If they ask for an added feature, it's tough to know if it will be of use to others as well. Today we have more customers, so it's easier to tell—from feedback—whether a requirement will meet more than one client's needs and to respond accordingly. That's an important ability start-ups must develop.

Entrepreneurs must also be fiscally conservative so they're ready for tough times. This skill actually helped us grow our business through the most recent recession. We have refused to over-leverage ourselves. The minute you take on a lot of debt, betting that you'll make X amount of sales, an economic downturn hits and you can't get through it.

New entrepreneurs can also be misinformed on the effort required to run a business. We see so many start-ups described as "overnight successes." Okay, it can happen, but it's extremely rare. The founders and others at Google, which some people believe came out of nowhere, worked long and hard before anyone realized what they were doing. Nulogy's "overnight success" took 10 years.

In fact, we've grown sales steadily throughout the latest recession. The market we serve has been fairly buoyant. For every small business in our customer base that didn't make it through, an equal or greater number of them are growing. Many big consumer goods companies are tightening their belts too, getting inventory off their balance sheets and outsourcing more work to stay lean. That outsourcing is the work that falls to our customers. In addition, a lot of the products packaged by our software are consumer staples that sell in almost any economic climate.

Because business is going well for us, we recently made the decision to raise $3 million in capital. We need to address a backlog of orders. We plan to use this money from Klass Capital to increase our product offerings, strengthen our customer service, and continue our expansion globally.

There are so many things we want to achieve. We can now think a lot more about the "future" projects we've always wanted to work on. A lot of our people are visionaries with great ideas. Now we'll have the chance to develop more of these ideas. It's a very exciting time.

Nulogy is all about the people. When we started out, the aim wasn't only to build a company that made "the most money ever," but also to create a great place to work. I still want to work with the best. We always hire people we feel are a good fit, who excel in their work, and with whom we'll enjoy working. It's a pleasure to come into the office when you know you'll have a good time, doing really great work with incredible people. And there's a new challenge every day.

Maybe it's entrepreneurial optimism speaking here, but I think we're all happy with how things have gone so far. We have many people to thank, of course—particularly our spouses, who, like us, have been willing to sacrifice so much in order to see our company succeed. There are long hours and calls and meetings to attend when we should be enjoying family time. It is a very tough balance.

When I tell friends, "I can't get away from work for very long today," they say, "But you're your own boss. You can do whatever you want." And to a certain extent it's true. In theory any of the founders could take a vacation anytime, but so much depends on us. Every day or hour we're away could mean critical work gets left undone. But really, the customer is always the boss, and this is particularly true for a company like ours. If a customer asks for an important task to be completed and we're not in the office, service will suffer.

I encourage budding entrepreneurs to look at real business problems and think, "Wouldn't it be better if things worked like this?" As the one in charge of our product design team, I see a huge emphasis from designers on solving small challenges and focusing on usability. That's fantastic, but there are problems that can't be solved that way; ones that are inherently complex. Don't discount their value. Not everything can be a mobile app.

I've been told by acquaintances, "I really want to start a business too. I'm just trying to find the right idea." My problem isn't a lack of ideas, it's that I have ideas all the time and although many could become businesses, I'm very busy with Nulogy right now. Even executing many more good Nulogy ideas is impossible because of time constraints.

You don't always get points for originality. Maybe your idea isn't new; it's just that no one's taken the time to nurture and execute it. I say take the time. It might be worth it.

16

TRAINING'S GREAT, BUT PERSEVERANCE LEADS TO GREATNESS

BENOIT LA SALLE
CEO, SEMAFO

"When people tell me an idea won't work, I know I'm onto something."

BENOIT LA SALLE

TYPE OF BUSINESS: *Gold mining companyr* | FOUNDED: *Montreal, Quebec, 1995*

www.semafo.com

WHEN I STARTED SEMAFO A LOT OF PEOPLE THOUGHT I WAS CRAZY. At the time I was a chartered accountant and the co-founder of a successful, independent accounting firm. I knew nothing about mining, but here I was running off to West Africa with a handful of mining permits, exploring for gold. As a CA, I was supposed to know all about risk, so what the heck was I doing?

I had multiple motives for making such a dramatic career change. First, I had promised to do everything I could to help the people of West Africa after visiting there in my role as a board member of a Canadian charity. Those people had put their faith in me, and I owed it to them to do everything I could to justify their faith. Naming our company SEMAFO, which in French is an acronym for West African Mining Corporation, was one tiny example of the lengths to which I want to go for the people of West Africa.

Second, my accounting partner, Yves Grou, and I really believed a gold mining venture made sense. Running a mining company requires many of the same organizational skills accountants develop, so we felt we were better suited to the task than other people believed. While some of our friends thought we were making a giant leap of faith, we knew we were taking a calculated risk that could pay off both emotionally and financially.

*   *   *

I learned at a relatively young age that when someone tells you something is impossible, a little perseverance can change everything. In 1977, I had just finished my CA exams and I wanted to pursue my MBA. I had applied to IMD International, an excellent university in Switzerland that accepts only 50 out of 2,500 applications each year.

I received a letter from IMD telling me I was too young to enter the MBA program and I would not be considered by the applications committee. The average age of IMD students was 36 and I was 22. Instead of giving up, I called IMD and told them they were making a mistake. I must have been on the phone for an hour trying to convince the registration people to allow my application to be considered.

My persistence paid off because IMD wrote back to me, saying that against their better judgment they were going to allow the committee to consider my application. IMD chose me as one of the 50 new students and I went on to finish my MBA at the university. This experience taught me to never give up, no matter what other people might think. This attitude helped me immensely in starting my own accounting practice, and then the mining company SEMAFO.

The first business I founded was my accounting firm, Grou La Salle & Associates. After I finished my MBA and articled, I decided I didn't want to follow the typical career path of joining one of the big accounting firms and working my way up the ladder. I wanted to start my own company and control my own career.

I decided to get advice from some of the top people in the big accounting firms before I set up my practice. Most of them told me an independent accounting firm would never succeed. They said a company needed to be big so it could have specialists in various fields, which would attract the most lucrative clients.

But again I persisted and, at 25, I founded Grou La Salle & Associates with my lifelong friend, Yves Grou. To make sure we had enough money to get through the early years, I applied for a teaching position at McGill University and unexpectedly got the job. So for 10 years I taught corporate finance as part of McGill's executive MBA program in addition to working at the accounting firm.

In 1993 I joined the board of Plan International Canada, a children's development organization dedicated to promoting children's rights and raising children out of poverty. The next year I travelled with the board to West Africa to visit some of our projects. At the time I was the francophone spokesperson for the organization and, since most of West Africa is French-speaking, I was making most of the presentations to senior officials and presidents.

Many of the senior officials I met indicated they would like to see Canadian companies come to West Africa because Canada has a lot of mining expertise. The West African countries believed they had a lot of mineral wealth, but they lacked the mining expertise to extract it. I told the officials I would see what I could do.

A year later, in 1995, I returned to West Africa with a geologist and we went to various West African countries where we obtained mining permits. I came back to Canada with the permits and with the goal of finding companies that would be willing to develop the sites. But I couldn't find anyone who wanted them. Africa in 1995 wasn't what it is today. There had been a lot of political coups in the 1980s and a lot of changes of governments. No one wanted to accept the risk of developing a mining site only to see a government overthrown and a new government voiding the permit. The companies I spoke with thought the situation in Africa was too unstable.

I had promised to help the West African governments and I wasn't going to give up. I had seen the poverty and it affected me deeply. I wanted to do anything I could to help better the lives of African civilians. So I talked to Yves and he thought a gold mining company might make sense. We decided to create our own company, SEMAFO, to try to develop the permits ourselves.

Of course people thought we were nuts. Here were two CAs who had articled with top accounting firms and had founded a successful accounting practice setting out to mine in West Africa, knowing nothing about geology or mining. From the reaction of some people you'd have thought we were launching an illegal casino.

But our accounting training gave us some principles and skills to run SEMAFO's operations. Mining companies are very financially oriented businesses and we were experts in finance and organization. The accounting firm also helped absorb miscellaneous expenses for SEMAFO, such as photocopying and mailing, which helped keep costs down.

West Africa was not a cheap place to operate and conditions there were difficult. For example, you couldn't leave a computer diskette sitting out on a desk in a room without air conditioning. It would warp and become unusable.

There were also a lot of travel and start-up expenses. We had to invest more than $100,000 of our own money, and back in 1995 that was a fortune. We began by setting up two shell companies and looking for funding.

When you are exploring potential mine sites there is no such thing as a small budget. You need skilled geologists, tools, mapping equipment, supplies, and money for long-distance travel. We estimated we would need $1 million for our first year of operation. So I went on the road to raise money, even though I had no experience. I spoke to people who had raised funds and I travelled to Montreal, Toronto, New York, London, Paris, and Zurich. In the end I think we raised around $600,000 from the first trip, so we were in good shape.

Our first round of funding in mid-1995 was made at 25 cents a share. We became very popular very quickly. By late 1996, our stock was over $10 per share. We were able to position ourselves as unique, which gave us some sex appeal in the market. We were French Canadian, we had mining experts on staff, and we were working in French-speaking Africa. We were also dedicated to helping the communities in which we operated.

Our timing was also good. When we started up there had been some recent natural resources success stories, like the Voisey Bay nickel mine in Labrador and Arequipa Resources Inc. in Peru, which was acquired by Barrick Gold for more than $600 million. The market was looking for the next big discovery and we were able to come in and ride the wave.

Recruiting people to go to West Africa was very tough in the beginning. It was unheard of to send people there. The logistics were incredibly difficult. Napoleon had a saying that you can't win a war without logistics, and it was true of Africa; you couldn't expect to succeed there in the mining business unless you planned well and were organized.

In a remote exploration camp there is no phone, no communication, and few roads. Fortunately for us, accounting requires a lot of structure, just like logistics. In the beginning we were far more focused on how we could buy what we needed and get it to the site so our team could focus on geology. We didn't want them worrying about where their food was going to come from. My belief was if we could provide a good bed, good food, and the proper tools, our people would work well for us and not want to leave at the first opportunity.

In the early days people had to be slightly maverick to work for us. They were going out into the jungle in the middle of nowhere to try to identify structures, outcroppings, and different types of rocks—anything that might make a promising mine. We needed special types of people to take on these assignments. Fortunately, we found some people who had experience working in the northern areas of Quebec who had no issues travelling to West Africa.

Everything was running very smoothly for us until 1997 when the Bre-X scandal hit. It was like someone turning off the lights. Our stock, which had been trading at $12 before the Bre-X scandal, plummeted to 15 cents. Bre-X shut down the resource sector until its revival in 2001.

Fortunately for us, we had just completed a $32-million round of funding one month before Bre-X. The timing really saved us and we had some money to see us through the tough times. Still, it was hard. We had to cut our team from over 200 people on exploration down to 15. We went into a care and maintenance mode and worked slowly on our projects.

Another thing that got us through the tough patch between 1997 and 2001 was sticking to our principles of helping the governments and people of West Africa. From 1998 to 2000, people were knocking on our door and telling us we should take the SEMAFO shell company and turn it into a high-tech company. High-tech was very hot and we had $32 million in our pockets.

We resisted. We had raised the money to mine natural resources. We also had a commitment to the countries where we operated and felt it was important to stick to our word. SEMAFO has corporate values and they're more than just words. We truly believe in those values.

It's a personal thrill to employ 2,200 individuals, of whom more than 2,000 are in Africa, and that for the majority of these people their positions at SEMAFO are their first jobs. In most cases they're probably the first people to have jobs in their families. In some cases they can be taking care of 20, 30, or 40 people because they have a salary. We pay them well. We provide education for their children and we provide work offers for their wives, because in many of the areas in which we operate, we run charities staffed largely by women. It's great to be able to say you make a difference, and we can say we make a difference in West Africa. It's what motivates me every day.

In 2009 we created the Fondation SEMAFO, a non-profit organization dedicated to helping the people of the countries in which SEMAFO operates, particularly in the areas of education and health. The foundation works on a range of projects, including one for the production and sale of sesame, and another for the building of a $2-million medical centre with surgical capabilities. It ships supplies such as books, pencils, blackboards, and clothes to schools and other needed supplies to hospitals and community projects. Two per cent of our annual after-tax profits go into the foundation, which makes a real difference in people's lives.

Our commitment to corporate responsibility helps to set us apart from other firms in Africa. We're a humanitarian mining company. We're seen by local governments as the company they want to deal with. This is very important.

But there are events we can control and those we can't. When we stuck to our principles during the lean period, it ultimately paid off. Bre-X may have turned off the lights for us, but the unfortunate terrorist attacks on the World Trade Center on September 11, 2001, turned them back on, and then some. On the morning of September 11, gold was at $260 an ounce. By the afternoon, it had already risen to $325. The uncertainty caused by the attacks and the new budget deficit policy of the U.S. caused the price of gold to keep moving up. People became much less likely to invest in U.S. dollars and more likely to invest in gold. We saw what was happening and I said, "This is it!" We put the turbo jets on, beefed up our exploration, and grew the company. In 2010 we had revenues of more than $320 million and were operating three gold mines in Burkina Faso, Niger, and Guinea.

Looking back, I don't think there's anything I would change about how we grew SEMAFO. The firm was started to help the people of West Africa and, by sticking to our principles, we have built a strong, successful company that gives back to communities. And it's not just the direct support we have given them through our company and charities. We have helped change the perception of businesses when it comes to West Africa. The region has the second best growth rate in the world, behind China. Some of the growth is the appeal of natural resources, but some of it is also because of us. Other businesses saw our success and realized if we could build a stable, profitable operation in West Africa, so could they.

When people tell me an idea won't work, I know I'm onto something. If I had listened to everyone who told me my ideas were crazy I never would have gone to IMD, I never would have co-founded an independent accounting practice, and SEMAFO would never have existed. I would say that the ideas people don't believe will work are the ideas that have changed the world. A lot of people aren't open-minded. They just want to build on what has been done in the past.

To be a true entrepreneur, you have to be willing to accept and promote change. This can be very difficult but, once you start, you become open-minded and willing to listen. Trailblazers are rarely given universally good feedback at the outset because they are seen as rocking the boat. When such entrepreneurs persevere and are successful, the skeptics tend to eventually quiet down—and what had long been considered impossible becomes a fixture of the competitive landscape.

17
FAMILY AND FORTITUDE

The Benefits of Creative Persistence

RAY PRICE

President, Sunterra Group

"Another 'people' challenge is running a family business.
That mantra of 'family is family and business is business' may have been
drilled into us at an early age, but it's easier said than done."

RAY PRICE

TYPE OF BUSINESS: *Meat processor, farmers* | FOUNDED: *Acme, Alberta, 1970*

www.sunterramarket.com

ONE OF THE MOST IMPORTANT LESSONS YOU LEARN growing up on a family farm in Western Canada is that when something needs doing, you do it. My five brothers, one sister, and I would split up the work, get out on the farm, and get it done. We also learned from a young age that family is family and business is business. Finally, we came to understand that when you're presented with a challenge, creative solutions are sometimes needed, especially when others are telling you your idea won't work. Our dad was always saying that.

In hindsight, I understand his motive. He was testing us. He knew by the time we hammered out all of the angles of an idea and considered every possible scenario, we'd know if it was worth the risk of going ahead. It certainly made us think in a sober way about our business decisions over the years.

Of course, Dad himself had always been on the leading edge, so it made us scratch our heads when he thought our ideas were crazy. Why weren't his own? I always thought he was the most critical guy I knew, but he was just teaching us to do our homework.

Our first opportunity to make a calculated business decision as a family came in the early 1970s. My father Stan and my mother Florence had been operating a farm in Acme, Alberta, for about 20 years. In 1962, my dad was approached by Ken Woolley, the founder of Pig Improvement Company (PIC) in England, who was spearheading change there and wanted to discuss pig genetics and how to improve breeding stock by identifying desirable traits.

My dad was well known on the pig side of the genetics business. In fact, Dr. Howard Fredeen, one of the leading geneticists in the world at that time, who was working out of Lacombe Research Station, and Dr. Jack Greenway, a veterinarian known for leading-edge health control systems, were friends of his. Together they all met with Woolley. Parts of the Canadian pig genetics business were technologically advanced relative to the rest of the world and Woolley wanted to know more about what we were doing.

After that initial consultation, Fredeen and Greenway continued to communicate with Woolley back in England to help develop the PIC business there. Then, in 1968, Woolley asked if anybody in our farming group wanted to learn about PIC. My brother Dave, the oldest, volunteered to go to England. When he returned two years later, he, my parents, Dr. Fredeen, and Dr. Greenway decided to launch Pig Improvement Canada, with PIC in England retaining 50 per cent ownership. The objective was to improve the quality of pigs in Canada.

Until that time, pure breeding was deemed the best way to produce pigs. But our science was saying that by crossbreeding you could retain the benefits of both breeds while injecting a measure of hybrid vigour, so the progeny would outperform the pure breed. This was the original concept behind Pig Improvement Canada: to use crossbred animals to produce higher quality pigs at a healthier and more efficient rate, converting feed into meat at a better rate than ever before.

It was such a novel concept that there were lots of doubters, and during our first four years in Canada many people refused to purchase our pigs. Normally, when buying a pig, you would attend a show where many of them were on display, simply picking ones that looked good. The PIC system was based on crossbreeding and the idea that in order to keep pigs healthy they needed to be isolated from other pigs, as well as from people. In fact, from the time we launched Pig Improvement Canada in 1970, no customer was able to enter the barns. They had to buy pigs based on their genetic merit, relying on information from a computer program specifically designed to calculate the value of a pig.

For the first four years, people said we were going to fail. Even PIC in England thought it might have made a mistake investing in the Canadian market. So, in 1973, knowing that PIC wanted out, my parents, Dave, Dr. Fredeen, and Dr. Greenway—joined by Woolley—bought back the 50 per cent retained by the UK company.

It was a very difficult time—that is, until we secured a few far-sighted customers. Within a couple of years those early customers were outperforming neighbouring farms and were breeding more pigs and generating more revenue for each. The word quickly spread. By the late 1970s our company was growing rapidly. In fact, by the middle of the 1980s, PIC was the largest pig breeding company in the world and Pig Improvement Canada was the leading supplier of pig genetics to the Canadian industry.

Many of the programs and methods that were considered unusual in the early 1970s are now standard practice. Back then, however, it took a lot of confidence to stick to them. We had to believe that by keeping our animals very clean we could more accurately measure their performance and make it easier to select the best ones. We were literally changing the face of pig production. The key was to develop the breeds at a very high level and then put the best two together to get that hybrid vigour. For example, crossing a Large White breed with a Landrace produces a breed that is very prolific (can produce a lot of pigs). Matching it with a breed with a very high level of lean meat without sacrificing much carcass gets you 50 per cent of the attributes of both—and a lean breed that reproduces more quickly.

We certainly had our own growing pains. In the early 1970s, pig prices were down. Even the grain side of the agricultural business was faring poorly. There were programs to cut grain production because there was such a surplus. Many producers exited the pig business during this time.

This worked to our advantage. Our crossbreeding process requires about three generations of livestock before commercial pigs are ready for market, so we needed those first few years to get going. By the time our first pigs were ready in 1973 many producers had left and demand was spiking. Of course we weren't completely ready. It takes two additional years to complete the next cycle. But this taught us a valuable lesson: you are always better off being a little short than a little long in the market. Certainly, in the 28 years we operated Pig Improvement Canada, there weren't too many times when we had more pigs than customers. We learned capacity is not as critical as having satisfied customers.

By 1979, when I joined the company full time, we had proven our breeding technology and the new business of hybrids. We were ready to expand. We were sending our pigs down to the U.S. and Mexico; we were dominating the Western Canadian market and were looking for opportunities in Eastern Canada. But when we went to Ontario, the biggest pig production zone in Canada at that time, we were once again met with naysayers.

Ontario was different from the West. Farmers relied on a more traditional system of pig farming and were reluctant to change. They resisted buying the new barns necessary to keep pigs separate. Looking back, I think it was another test that we passed.

Not long after I started, we built a new facility to supply genetics to Ontario and Quebec. My brother Dave concentrated on marketing in Quebec while I went back and forth to Ontario, organizing a new customer base. The pure-bred business was well established in Ontario and the provincial government was still a powerful influence on the industry. Even though our technology was 10 years old, it was considered new. Many farmers compared us to other companies that tried to do the same thing but had cut corners. It took us a little longer than expected, but eventually some of the leading producers in Ontario started to use our genetics.

I guess you could say the Price family isn't afraid of new challenges. We just put a lot of hard work into it. It dates back to those early days on the farm when we simply did what needed to be done. When I came into the company, another one of my responsibilities was to build a genetic evaluation program to demonstrate the merit of our pigs. At first we were sending our data to the University of Calgary mainframe for processing, but it was a three-day turnaround and, because it was a card-based system, if one of the cards had an incorrect entry, the system would kick them all out.

My dad thought it would be easier to train somebody from agriculture how to program than it would be to train a computer programmer about agriculture, so I became his guinea pig. One of my first jobs at Pig Improvement Canada was to write software for an indexing system to determine the generic merit of each of our crossbreeds. He set me up on a Model One Radio Shack computer and it was supposed to be a temporary part-time gig. I guess you could say it evolved into a little more.

Back then, our computer program was so new it caught the attention of other companies, who started to replicate it. It was a pretty exciting time. We were watching the industry evolve, knowing our company was playing a small part in a global transition.

By the mid-1980s, we realized selling pig genetics alone wasn't enough. We saw our meat in the stores and we always knew it was better than average, but we wanted to understand the meat-packing side of the business. We knew that if we could get more meat to consumers, they would prefer it, and that in turn would help our breeding stock sales. We spent quite a lot of time understanding this market perspective and, in 1989, decided to invest in a small meat-processing facility.

Our new business, Trochu Meat Processors Ltd., was also one of the first meat packers in Canada to hire a meat scientist. We did genetic evaluations and carcass cut-outs to determine the value of a carcass. Still, we were quite naive about the industry. In 1990, when we bought the plant, it could only sell in Alberta because it was a provincially inspected plant. It was small too. We were only processing 300 head per week.

But we wanted to open up stores and sell the meat from our plant into our stores, generating our own customer base. When we purchased the meat-packing facility in 1990, we also launched our Sunterra Markets store at Bankers Hall in downtown Calgary—a full-service store with in-house chefs, fresh food, and high-quality meats at a time when retailers had super stores with no service and low-cost and yellow label products. We modelled our store after European markets where food is purchased for freshness. Industry people were not encouraging. They said, "Don't you see which way the whole industry is moving?"

By the time the banker told us it was a bad idea, we had already done enough homework to know we were onto something. We adopted an attitude of "we'll show you."

That's not to say we didn't run into some snags. We realized early that loin and tenderloin were very popular fresh meats but that ham and bellies were not. In order to get more of the loins we had to process more pigs, generating more of the meat products for which we didn't have a market.

*   *   *

In 1993, a customer from the genetics side of our company came to us with an opportunity in Japan. He had a contact there who was looking for good pork. So we changed our meat packing facility to federal inspection, packaged our first load, and shipped it overseas. Our Japanese client was very satisfied with our meat but said we didn't know what we were doing when it came to meat-packing.

I spent a lot of time going back and forth to Japan with some of our team to understand what they wanted. I remember one of our first meetings very clearly. They asked us what we produced and our reply was, "Whatever you want." We went back and forth with the interpreter three or four times before they finally understood we would deliver whatever they wanted. If we were selling a product, we'd be like everybody else. We were selling a service, and this was one of our key differentiators. The message got through.

We started to slowly grow our Japanese business, and by 1996 we had expanded our plant to produce chilled pork rather than frozen. The market in Japan was starting to evolve and we felt it was important to provide a fresh product that would be more valuable to our customers there. Many Japanese visitors came over to inspect our plant and our processes to ensure we could produce the quality they desired. One visitor was adamant we would never sell fresh pork to Japan, let alone product to his company. We kept working to our goal of increasing sales to Japan by visiting the company, providing samples, and following up on every detail. Our product in Japan became known for its quality, and we became known for our ability to meet our customers' requirements.

About two years after the visitor pronounced we would not be successful, we started a weekly business with the company he worked for in a deal that has generated more than $50 million in sales. He is no longer with the company. Japan has evolved into our best market and over 70 per cent of our pork sales are to customers there.

Over the years many of our employees have travelled to Japan to learn more about our customers' businesses and requirements. It has been a highlight to travel with them and watch them take in a new culture and new experiences. I know our customers appreciate the contact and the opportunity to interact with our staff, and it has helped us to make the necessary changes so we can consistently deliver the best possible product to them.

Venturing into Japan also drew more attention to our pigs and what we could do with them. Our customers taught us a great deal about quality and food safety. We learned how to handle and package the pork to keep it cold and safe, so we could provide a chilled pork product for Japanese supermarkets that was just as good as their locally sourced products. We learned which pig nutrition could produce the highest quality pork for both Japan and our own market. We ship a container a day and sell 10 times the amount of pork than when we first started out. There are nine Sunterra Market food stores.

*   *   *

The growth of our business on the retail side, combined with our processing business, allowed us to sell the breeding stock business in 1998. Though it was our core and long-term business, we believed demand and volume had peaked in Canada. By trying to increase the market share of Pig Improvement Canada, we would reduce our profitability by cannibalizing our own sales. One thing we did retain, however, was the breeding stock and the genetics. Our unique set of genetics had proven highly successful in Japan and we wanted to keep it going.

The decision was pretty dramatic, but after 28 years in the business operating under the worldwide umbrella of PIC, the future didn't look bright. Having a pig production side to our business made our decision to sell a little bit easier, but it was a major departure for us. I give a lot of credit to my dad and my brother Dave who had developed that part of the business and recognized when to get out of it. A lot of entrepreneurs hang on until it's too late.

One of my greatest personal thrills as a business owner came during this time. As part of our redirection and renewed focus on the retail and meat-processing side of our business, we offered our shareholders the chance to sell their shares. The Woolley family and Dr. Fredeen were still involved; we wanted to create some liquidity for some of our long-time investors. They said they didn't want out. To me, that was a great feeling, because it showed that the partnership worked. You don't often see that kind of loyalty in a private company with an 80 per cent family majority.

We've been fortunate to have high-calibre employees throughout our organization right from the start. Our people inspire my passion for the business. I love watching their evolution and growth, and, in some cases, I think they're more excited about our business than we are. We think of them as part of our family.

Examples of their dedication are evident throughout our business. When we opened our Sunterra Food Market at Bankers Hall everyone pitched in, including our admin team. Our CFO and our marketing manager were there all night mopping floors, stocking shelves, and pricing product. That evening we had a preview opening for the employees in the building and expected about 500 people. Over 1,000 attended, and the Market is successfully operating 21 years later.

Another time, we renovated a store we had recently purchased so it would have the look and feel of our other Sunterra stores. We decided we could only have the store closed for 10 days. We were concerned that if we were closed much longer than that, customers would find other places to shop. My brother Glen must have spent 200 of the 240 hours at the store keeping ahead of, or motivating, the contractors. It seemed everything that could happen did, including one of the contractors actually cutting through the main power supply with a saw. No one was hurt, but it did shut down the whole building, including the vault in the Royal Bank sharing the first floor next to our store. Despite this being a contractor mistake, it was left to our staff to visit the bank and make sure everyone there knew we were doing what we could to fix the problem. When the store reopened after 10 days, we invited everyone from the bank and all the other neighbours to see the changes. Practically every square foot of the store had been changed, and seeing the results of the construction made it much easier for them to understand what the disruption and extra noise had been about.

One of our more recent store openings involved trying to get the computer register system operating properly. Data seemed to be missing, so teams of people took every item in the store to the admin office in order to scan the product and verify that it was in the system properly and had the right description. Some of the team worked through the night, and one employee fell asleep at about 5:45 A.M. with his face leaning against a shopping cart. When he awoke, the cross-hatch of the shopping-cart bars was stencilled in red on his cheek. It helped lighten the mood, and by 7:00 A.M. when the local TV morning show came to film at the store for the opening, everything was ready—although he declined to go on camera for an interview.

Yet, just as much as our relationships have been rewarding, they've also been challenging, particularly on the financial side. In the early 1970s when we were getting into pig genetics, it was such a new concept that the banks didn't know what to make of it. We were fortunate to be working with a good agricultural banker at the time. Without that relationship, I don't know whether we could have achieved what we did. Business relationships and dealings have changed so much over the years. There's a lot more legal paperwork now. You used to be able to tell bankers how you planned to execute a plan. Today we often hear, "It's not in the contract." I spend way more time on contracts than what is necessary or prudent.

*   *   *

Our first banking relationship lasted 23 years, the second lasted 10, and our next one lasted four. The pattern is not so much a reflection of how we changed, but how systems have changed. I think these are the questions facing new entrepreneurs: Where does the money come from? How do I manage the money? How do I sell my concept?

How do I stick with it? And, how do I know the banker providing the money will be there a year from now?

We learned that people and directions change. One day your bank manager can be very focused on agriculture and a year later he/she will be onto a different sector. At the same we were growing, the banking sector was pulling back. If there is any one segment of the industry the banks don't like, we are probably in it, by combining agriculture, meat-packing, and retail. At one point, a banker told us that he had determined the biggest part of our business to be in real estate. We didn't have a lot of real estate; it was farmland. Nonetheless, because our land holdings were large, the banker was going to shuffle us over to the Commercial Real Estate department. We were forced to get a deal elsewhere.

I've learned we don't ever want to be in a position where the banks are telling us what to do. Entrepreneurs, us included, don't like to give up equity. The idea is to work with banks to leverage your equity, and it boils down to your interaction and relationships with people. Sometimes, just when things are going great, your representative retires and the new guy brings along a whole new set of rules.

Another "people" challenge is running a family business. That mantra of "family is family and business is business" may have been drilled into us at an early age, but it's easier said than done. In our case, we're brothers and we've always found answers to problems. In the beginning, my brother Glen was reluctant to get involved in the business so we spent some time talking about it, examining difficulties and challenges. My brother Al and sister Joyce have never been actively involved in the business except as small shareholders and consumers. Dave is the chairman of the board, I'm president, Glen is the president of Sunterra Markets, while Doug is on the board and has a cattle operation that provides beef for our Sunterra Markets. Art is chair of the executive committee. We all have varying levels of ownership. My mom, who is in her eighties, is still involved and produces the company newsletter. Despite my original job of programming computers, she is much more proficient with her Mac. In fact she was the first one in the family to have an iPad.

About 10 years ago we had to sit down and have a serious discussion about how the third generation would be brought into the Sunterra Group. Part of our mission was to make them aware of the trials they would face if they joined. We also wanted to lay down some ground rules. For one, they would have to work from the ground up, and they wouldn't receive special treatment. If they wanted a job, they would have to apply for it. The one thing we warned them about is no matter what, people will think they were hired because they're related. This perception means they will have to prove their worthiness. Each of us has had to prove our value, and it's the same for them.

My brothers and I have always managed to get along, but the transition to the next generation worries us a bit. I know in my own case, I worked in the same 10-foot-by-15-foot office as my dad for about five years when I first started out. He smoked and I didn't, and it just about drove me nuts. But that's just part of growing up in a big family—you put up with some of those things.

Dave and I have worked side by side for the past 31 years. We've always tended to take on different roles. We can rely on each other. Glen has been responsible for Sunterra Markets since the start in 1990 and, while we might have discussions and the odd argument, I know he is the expert. It doesn't stop me from telling him what I think, but at the end of the day we trust each other to make good decisions.

As members of the Canadian Association of Family Enterprises, we're more aware of problems that can occur in a family business. But while a brother's bond is very close, can a parent–child bond be stronger? The risk is that it could be. We're trying to reward our children based on merit, and we're trying to teach them that nobody has an automatic right to be part of the business. So far, our kids are all happy doing what they're doing. Sometimes my own kids tell me I work too hard and I should have more fun. They don't realize work is fun for me.

*   *   *

After 40 years in business we have made a few mistakes, but my dad would say, "Just don't make any mistake twice." If you don't get out there and try things, you'll never learn what works.

My dad passed away in April 2010, but I like to think his legacy lives on in our family business—a legacy of calculated risks and a certain bull-headedness.

I'm reminded of the time when we were launching the first Sunterra Food Market at Bankers Hall in Calgary. We knew we wanted to be on the second floor where the foot traffic was and to have an open storefront so people would see our chefs preparing succulent meals each day. We had these two big cooking pans, three feet across, and we were counting on the aromas to draw people in. The mall owners allowed our open storefront but didn't want those big metal folding doors to our shop to close up at night. They thought it would look tacky. They wanted us to use glass instead and they even offered to pay for installation.

At the end of our first night we were trying to shut these big glass doors and there was a little bit of a cement rise that was preventing them from closing. We had to take the doors right off and put them back on, but Glen and I knew it would be a problem the next day. So we went out and rented a jackhammer and the next morning, bright and early, went to work to jackhammer the ridge in the concrete that was stopping the doors from moving properly on their track. You can imagine the noise we were making on the second floor of this office building with other retail outlets all around us. Of course it took a little longer than we thought, and at 8:10 A.M. we were still at it, hammering away.

When the building manager suddenly came by we expected to get some static. The area we were working on at the time was in a small closet about 4 feet by 6 feet and we had the door closed. When he opened the door you could tell he was going to say something, but he saw it was Glen and me, looked us over for a minute, then said "Oh, it's you guys," shook his head and just walked away.

It was one of those times where if we had asked to do it, it wouldn't have gotten done. We knew it was better to ask for forgiveness than permission. In the end, he was just as happy as we were to see the problem resolved.

That's the way it is in our family. It always has been. Family may be family and business may be business, but when something needs doing, you better not be afraid to get in there and do it—no matter what others might say.

18
A MIND FOR NUMBERS, A HEART FOR PEOPLE

STEVE GUPTA
President and CEO, Easton's Group of Hotels

"I tell my children, 'A good reputation can earn you money,
but with money you cannot build a good reputation.'"

STEVE GUPTA

TYPE OF BUSINESS: *Real estate developer, hotelier* | FOUNDED: *Port Hope, Ontario, 1979*

www.eastonsgroup.com

EVER SINCE I WAS A YOUNG BOY GROWING UP in India I had this feeling I was going to do something big. I just didn't know what it would be or exactly how I would do it. The one thing I did know was I would always use my head for numbers and my heart for people. Connecting with people is half the battle in business. I honestly believe that if you are sincere, honest, and devoted, you'll never have any problems. Of course, that doesn't mean you can be naive. I always gauge the sincerity in every person I meet and when it's not there, I act accordingly.

I first arrived in Canada in 1971, settling in Toronto. Back home, my father had a successful construction business and, as his eldest son, I was expected to carry on. But my heart said differently. I wanted to have something on my own, to start my own life, and I simply told myself it was time to go and do what I really wanted to do. After working in Canada for a year, I went back to India to get married, returning in 1973 with my young and beautiful bride by my side.

My first job was selling insurance for North American Life. Even then I was always searching for the big business opportunity, but I didn't have the money. So I started the numbers game—wheeling and dealing in real estate to try to accumulate investment capital. Finally, I had $15,000 in the bank and I was ready.

In 1978, I met with a gentleman who had leased a gas station in Toronto's east end and wanted someone to assume the balance of the lease. We agreed on a price of $15,000 with a $1,500 deposit. It was my first business deal and it was scribbled on the back of a pink message slip. But then he got greedy and reneged. I was disappointed, but the way I saw it, if somebody was going to tell me I couldn't do something then I was simply going to prove that I could do it—and more.

A little while later, I was perusing the *Toronto Star* and I happened to notice an advertisement posted by a real estate agent saying, "If you have $15,000 I have a gas station for sale for you." So I called him. I quickly surmised that his ad was a gimmick to generate new clients. He started asking me how much money I had, trying to size me up. He said if I had $100,000 then he had something "really good." I knew I had less than one-sixth of that amount but I played his game anyway, requesting more information.

Of course I didn't hear from the agent after that meeting. But about two or three days later, I called him back, looking for the information. To say he gave me the runaround is an understatement. At first he was on "standby," waiting for an update on the $100,000 opportunity. Then the story changed; he had reached his contact, scribbled the numbers down, but had thrown the slip of paper away. I had a hunch so I kept digging, eventually learning that the gas station in question was a popular truck stop off Highway 401 at Highway 28 near Port Hope, Ontario.

It turned out two of the founders of the truck stop were looking to sell. When they found out the prospective buyer was from Toronto, the $100,000 fee quickly turned into $300,000 on a $1.3-million business. I told the agent it was way too much but to arrange a meeting anyway.

Thinking back, I realized they didn't really want to meet with me at the service centre. Our appointment took place at the home of one of the vendors. I was trying to figure out how interested they really were in selling and they were sizing me up at the same time. Needless to say, they weren't pleased with my initial offer of $750,000 and tried to get my agent to apply pressure. To make a long story short, we sealed the deal at $950,000 for $200,000 down, with the vendors agreeing to hold a $508,000 second mortgage for seven years from 2 per cent to 7 per cent staggered, and a first mortgage of approximately $240,000, held by Texaco Canada.

To this day, I can swiftly pull these numbers out of my memory bank. My two years of study in mathematics toward a master's degree helped, and I've always enjoyed working with numbers. In my head I had quickly worked it out and, believing I could really do something with this property—and with God's grace—I simply made it happen. Soon after I got two friends to join me as partners at 31 per cent each and I took the remaining 38 per cent. Four months later, one partner opted out for a $14,000 return on his initial investment of $66,000, leaving me with 60 per cent control and my remaining partner with 40 per cent.

The vendors, as it turned out, were excellent business people. They had built their company on the basis of providing fantastic service and customers kept coming back. They also had good overall business relationships in place. But I knew if I was going to do something really special with the location, I needed to increase my numbers.

Sitting down with a very senior officer from Texaco, I made my case. And, true to my style, I spoke from my heart, telling him I could increase his business if he provided me with a volume discount. We worked out a deal and in no time I had increased my margins from $0.03 per litre to nearly $0.06, using my savings to attract more trucking companies to my location. At the same time, I made my self-serve diesel more attractive by providing attendants to top up windshield wiper fluid and clean windshields. This is how we built our business, and our numbers at the cafeteria-style on-site restaurant also started to increase.

In those early days, I would wake at 4:45 A.M. six days a week in order to make the trek to Port Hope in time for a 7:00 A.M. start. My partners took care of Sundays. It was a gruelling schedule, to say the least, and after one year my remaining partner also decided to get out.

Then, three months after buying out my partner to become sole owner, I was approached out of the blue by the founders to purchase the second mortgage they held on the property. Right away, my wheels started to turn. I asked for 48 hours to see what I could do.

That night I went home and performed my magic with the numbers, working out my present values for seven years by hand and calculating what the discount should be. In the end, I purchased the $508,000 mortgage back at a discount which I was now able to finance with a bank loan.

One of the lessons I learned very early on in my business dealings is to examine all of the angles so you can uncover the one thing that perhaps somebody else has missed. As sole owner of the truck stop, I upgraded the 10 rooms we had for truck drivers to sleep during stopovers, providing them with clean towels and soap so they could shower. We put new beds in, made a TV lounge, and we started running at 70 per cent occupancy, Monday through Friday. I may not have realized it at the time, but this was the start of what would eventually grow into a highly successful hotel enterprise.

*　　*　　*

The more I considered the angle of a hotel for my 10-acre site in Port Hope, the more I realized that if I could start selling alcohol I could really increase my earnings, as just south of us was the town of Port Hope. But my location in Hope Township, a town of 4,000 people, was a designated dry area. I joined forces with another local restaurant owner and together we lobbied for change, paying someone $10,000 to go door-to-door to sway public opinion in our favour. We were successful in changing the law but I held off on introducing liquor into my restaurant as the waitresses were not ready to work in a licensed environment. It was one of those times when my heart prevailed and out of respect for my employees, who were dead set against it, I waited.

In 1987, nearly a decade after purchasing the Port Hope truck stop, I decided to approach Cara Operations Ltd. about the possibility of putting a Swiss Chalet and Harvey's at my location. We held many meetings over the course of several months and finally I found myself face to face with six vice-presidents from head office. They were presenting their case for not doing it when finally I said, "Let me ask you one question before I leave. How many times have you guys kicked yourselves when you lost a really good deal?" They all smiled and one of them responded, "A few." To which I replied, "Add one more to your list."

I guess you could say I really didn't like to be told I couldn't do something. Refusing to take no for an answer, I convinced them the majority of the risk was mine and the only investment they needed to make was their flag. Maybe I was a bit pushy, but thought that in hindsight they would thank me, maybe even wish I had been more adamant. They eventually agreed to put a scaled-down version of their restaurants at my location, and before long we had earned a position among the top 10 Swiss Chalet locations in Canada based on per-seat sales. And our Harvey's was number one in breakfast sales.

Soon after, I used my newfound success to expand further, putting a Comfort Inn franchise on part of the 10 acres of land that housed the truck stop. All of a sudden a million-dollar business became a $10- to $15-million dollar operation and I couldn't stop thinking about how far I still wanted to go after my humble start with only $15,000.

I was also diversifying into real estate. I still recall my first apartment building deal in the early spring of 1983 with the President of Sealy Mortgage Corp. My broker was very impressed with my approach, and I started to buy more apartment buildings.

Then in January 1986, late at night, I got a call from a real estate agent who would once again put my penchant for numbers to the test. He was having drinks with somebody from a management company who was trying to put together a multimillion-dollar bid on 2,500 apartment units and the bid was closing the next day. So I got this call and I said, "Okay. Come on over to my house. Let me look at the numbers."

I sat down with them from 12:30 A.M. to 4:00 A.M., going over the numbers. I believe that I'm very, very good with numbers and acquisition is my expertise. Not to brag, but in those days, I even fielded calls from appraisers asking me what I thought a certain property in Toronto was worth. Anyway, on the night in question I made a deal to bid together with the management company, provided that I could set the price and the split would be 50/50.

Just two hours after we parted, a representative came to take me to visit the properties. There were 600 units in Hamilton, more than 1,000 in Brampton, and a few more in Toronto. By 10:00 A.M. I was back at the office. The offers were already sitting there, ready for me, and I filled in my figure: $59.7 million with less than a 12 per cent cash down payment. We structured the deal similarly to the way I structured my bid for the Eastons' gas station. Another bidder challenged our offer, claiming to have a higher bid. But they had based their price on a clause to buy back the vendor take-back mortgage at a discount, and they wanted to withdraw that clause. To make a long story short, they took us to court where our original bid held up and on June 12, 1986, we closed the deal and purchased 2,500 apartment units.

*   *   *

At the same time, Clarkson Gordon, as receiver, was accepting bids on a number of Cadillac Fairview portfolios. I didn't have money at the time, having just completed the $59.7-million deal, but I believed my fate would soon change due to my recent purchase. I wrote a letter expressing my interest in the portfolios and requesting more time to bid—in a nutshell we asked them to postpone the bidding date. I don't know if it was because of me, or maybe other people were asking for the same thing, but it worked; they postponed the bidding.

The lesson here is to look into every possibility. Unleash the will of your soul and the soul decides its goal. If you don't know enough about something, find the consultant or specialist who can give you sound advice so you can make informed decisions. I've always done my research. If you tell me two plus two equals four, I'll accept it, but then I'll dig further so that I understand why it should be four.

After writing the letter requesting more time, I approached my partners and asked them how they would feel to see a headline in the *Toronto Star* reading, "No-Names Buy Cadillac Fairview Properties." Once again, the numbers were flowing in my mind. We paid $59.7 million, but I figured we could sell the same portfolio for $80 million if they just gave me three months. Trusting in me, they allowed me to restructure, repositioning our wholesale purchase to sell off each building individually. The way I see it, it's about making your package look pretty, whatever it is you are trying to sell. If I go to the bank to borrow money, I need to convince them about the integrity of my project. If I'm trying to sell a building, I need to make it look attractive, even if it means raising rents.

By September 1986, we had flipped the buildings for a $20-million profit, just as I had predicted. We now had the influx of cash and I was asked to spearhead the group bidding on the Cadillac Fairview properties.

On February 28, 1987, around the same time I was talking to Cara Corp. about expanding my truck stop, we succeeded in purchasing 5,726 of the 10,931 Cadillac Fairview holdings for $209 million. This was one of my proudest moments. Here I was, a guy who had arrived in the country 15 years earlier with $108 to my name, making a multimillion-dollar acquisition. People may have wondered, "Who is this guy?"—and rightfully so.

Some people say I'm lucky. There is some truth to this, but what luck brings you is opportunity. I always say opportunity knocks at your door. If you don't open the door to let it in, it's going to go and knock on someone else's door. As much as these early opportunities came my way, I also made them happen, relying on passion, drive, and my willingness to put in a lot of hard work. The harder I worked, the luckier I got.

I've been called a walking encyclopedia, but I'm really not Mr. Know-It-All. I just pay attention and my mind is like a huge sponge. I truly believe my education was my foundation and know I'm building an enormous pool of knowledge on top of it with my experience, layer by layer and story by story. That's how I get by.

Now, I have made mistakes and weathered my share of troubles over the years, but I have always persevered. And I wouldn't call them mistakes; I'd call them missed opportunities. I like to say if I had capitalized on all those missed opportunities, the outcome may have changed. You have to remember that when I came to this country I had nothing, so rolling properties was the best way to get cash in my hands. But hindsight can be 20/20. There are a few properties that I owned near Bathurst Street and Steeles Avenue in Toronto; if instead of selling them I had sat on them, like people who had money were able to do, I would be sitting on properties worth $40 million today. So you do kick yourself sometimes.

At the same time, I feel fortunate to have had the foresight to plan for difficult times. During the early 1990s, when the NDP government came into power in Ontario and passed a law to roll back rent increases retroactively on all apartment buildings, some people were wiped out. I lost $5 million in net income per year but in order to weather the storm I borrowed $4 million against my Port Hope property, keeping $4 million in the bank. And, believe me, I used it all, because I had to feed all the negative cash flows.

I also had to weather adversity during 9/11 and in 2007 and 2008. Just prior to the past recession, I repositioned and refinanced some of my properties. I borrowed somewhere around $15 to $20 million with plans to start some projects, so the money was just sitting there. The tough decision I had to make was whether or not to go ahead. The recession was imminent and everyone else was standing still.

I guess I'm a contrarian. I went against the tide and built. Construction was slow, prices were low, and in 2008 I built two downtown hotels, both of them requiring approximately $100 million in construction costs.

Then in 2009 I built another three, three more in 2010, and in 2011 we plan to build two more hotels and an office building. Going against the tide, I was able to save 25 per cent on construction costs.

If I can give a piece of advice to people, it's to diversify. I've always kept my eggs in different baskets, not just one. I always have income-producing properties like my gas stations and Swiss Chalets and I've always kept them at a distance from my company. Another tip is that I've always kept my loan-to-value ratio below 65 per cent. If I need $10 million for a project, I'll register for $15 million so the extra $5 million is sitting there in case I need it. Like I've always said, there's a different angle for everything, even accounting.

*   *   *

Business is a numbers game, and how fast you act is what makes the difference. I'm fortunate to be pretty good at making split-second decisions. But in order to grow and buy bigger projects you also need to access money from others, and that's where the heart comes in. Where there's money and power involved there can also be greed, and that's how people get into trouble.

I speak from my own mind and my own heart. I don't make speeches to impress people. I always bring sincerity to my relationships, whether it's business, personal, or family. I have 1,400 people working for me now and I like to think I'm hands-on, down-to-earth, one of those presidents who are willing to roll up their shirt-sleeves to pitch in and get their hands dirty.

One time there was a housekeeper in one of my hotels who was struggling to lift a night table. I happened to be there so I lifted it up and put it on the trolley, and then told her to let me get the other one as well. She almost had tears in her eyes. But that's the human touch I believe in.

It's important to have your feet firmly grounded. That's what I work on and what I teach my children. I want them to feel the same sense of pride I do in knowing that I've contributed to my country, Canada, and am building a good name. That's very important to me. I tell my children, "A good reputation can earn you money, but with money you cannot build a good reputation." I've left money on the table for many deals, many times, when the only other choice would create animosity.

Finally, like I've said before, I may be good at crunching numbers to seal a deal but I wouldn't be where I am today if I didn't have the unconditional support of my wife and children.

19
A BILLION AND BACK

How a Leap Forward in Electronics Miniaturization Breathed Life into a Business Idea

PAUL WALKER

Owner and Chief Executive Officer, Artaflex Inc.
Founder, Surface Mount Technology Centre Inc.

"When someone tells me my idea is not going to work I always ask them, 'How do kites rise?' I tell them, 'Kites rise against the wind. You can't get a kite to rise if you're going with the wind.' When people tell you something will never work, it means you're going against the wind. If everyone else is doing it, you have to do it differently."

PAUL WALKER

TYPE OF BUSINESS: *Electronics contract manufacturer* | FOUNDED: *Markham, Ontario, 1985*

www.artaflex.com

IN THE EARLY 1980s, WHILE WORKING AT MOTOROLA, I had the experience of working with a manufacturing innovation called surface mount technology (SMT). I felt it was going to gain acceptance quickly and just had to be a part of the development wave that was sure to follow. Clearly I needed to start a company, but my understanding of how to wrap a workable business concept around this giant leap forward in electronics technology was still foggy.

SMT allows miniaturization in electronics. None of today's electronics products could be as small as they are without this technology, which in essence allows components to be mounted directly on the surface of the printed circuit board (hence the name surface mount), opening up a significant amount of space in an area where space is undeniably at a premium.

The "brick," that giant cell phone with the clunky charger that business people carried around almost 30 years ago, is of course long gone and amazingly light mobile phones smaller than our hands have taken its place. Smartphones, including BlackBerry, iPhone, and Android devices, are actually mini-computers, while today's incredibly thin tablet PCs offer extremely high-definition displays and processing power. Products like microwave ovens or electronics found in car dashboards have also made dramatic ergonomic improvements. None of this would have happened without SMT.

Of course, as a young, naive, 25-year-old entrepreneur, I thought the whole world was going to want this technology and all they had to do was see it. When you are inexperienced you tend to jump into the fray before you are ready—even before finishing all your market research. That was me.

But with ample confidence in the future of the technology, I got out there and started trying to sell the manufacturing equipment to both the original equipment manufacturers (OEMs) and contract assemblers so they could produce the technology. At least, that was the intention!

I found out very quickly that the few companies doing assembly work weren't really used to buying new equipment for new technology before they had the orders. They were mature companies with their own equipment and they had done this type of work using through-hole technology for years. Their basic premise was,

"We'll wait, and when we see some demand for SMT we might buy the equipment from you."

We heard the same answer over and over and, as a result, there were no sales and I was starving. However, in a backward way, I was actually gathering my market research as I learned no one in this country was prepared to go out on a limb and buy the SMT equipment before they had the demand.

I knew right then that the person or company going first would gain a stranglehold on the market.

*   *   *

The idea for our company, SMTC (which stood for Surface Mount Technology Centre Inc.), was actually formed by me and two partners, Gary and Derek (Phil joined later). We sketched it out on a napkin after another day without a sale. The thought was to try to capture the Canadian market by purchasing the equipment, putting it in a building, and promoting the use of SMT.

We would not just be equipment representatives anymore; we would also offer a training centre for people who wanted to learn more about SMT. The thought was that people or companies who got comfortable with the technology would then design it onto their boards.

We started training engineers and designers from almost every major OEM, such as IBM, Northern Telecom, Mitel, Ford, and Motorola, on how they could take a through-hole board, maybe one foot by one foot, and miniaturize it to six inches by six inches. We knew they would ultimately buy our equipment or outsource the manufacturing to us. It was either option A or B.

Though our plan was confirmed on a napkin, as I said, we subsequently put a comprehensive business plan together. Significant work went into writing it, justifying it, figuring out the return, and making additional plans and projections. But that's where we hit our first roadblock.

The original business plan called for us to raise $400,000. I'm sure we weren't the first entrepreneurs to believe our company was going to take off and everyone would see things our way, but when you start meeting with bankers you quickly realize that's not the case.

We approached all the major banks and learned they don't fund start-ups. They don't take risks. We then approached most of the venture capital, private equity-type groups in Canada, but back in 1985 the market was not particularly mature. And we were surprised to learn they weren't interested either.

It was funny because they didn't dislike our plan; they just said it was too small. I didn't understand it at the time, but it meant they would have to put the same money into due diligence, lawyers, accountants, paperwork—really the same general effort into a $400,000 deal as they would on a $4-million deal, or even a $40-million deal. It was just more zeros to them.

Since neither the banks nor private equity investors would help us, the dream died. We couldn't raise the money.

We couldn't move forward and we were licking our wounds. Then one day I was up at the family cottage on the dock, dangling my feet in the water and feeling rotten. My dad came down to the end of the dock and asked me what was wrong.

I told him how the deal failed because we couldn't raise the money. When I told him how much we needed, he asked if we might be able to get started with less. He and Mom didn't have $400,000 but if we reconsidered the plan he said they'd see if they could help.

We scaled back our vision a bit. We found a way to dig into whatever savings we had and borrow the equipment. We thought we could survive for six months with only $50,000.

I told my father. Two or three weeks later he came back and said, "Where do you want the money deposited? Your mom and I are going to lend you the $50,000 for your dream." I was initially taken aback, not keen to put them at risk, but they weren't about to change their minds.

We took the money and put our new plan into action. I didn't know until later that my parents had remortgaged their house. If I'd known that I definitely would have refused to take the money.

Still, I suppose their support was not a complete shocker. One of the partners was my brother, the others were best friends, and we all had worked in engineering at Motorola Canada under my dad, who ran manufacturing there. Familiarity holds a lot of sway in business—especially among lenders—since people don't invest in businesses, they invest in people. I've learned this lesson over the last 30 years, during which I have raised hundreds of millions of dollars, but my parents provided the first illustration of the rule.

SMTC got up and running in the summer and we had enough money to last until Christmas. It was slow going, which is nerve-racking when you have limited time to show success, but we actually got our first significant cheque from a customer just before Christmas. If we hadn't, we would have run out of money and been forced to start all over again.

We kept our costs down by filling our demo room with loaner equipment from the companies we were representing. The SMT manufacturers knew if they put equipment in our labs and we trained engineers on it, these engineers would buy the equipment when the time came that they felt comfortable using it. Out of the $400,000 in our business plan, the cost of the equipment was about $350,000.

So we survived, and, over the next few years, word spread about SMTC, both in Canada and the United States.

There were a few operational steps we had to take after this growth phase. Five to seven years in, we were still four partners without titles on our business cards. One of the hardest things to do—especially among friends and relatives in their twenties—is to assign responsibility. But it's also impossible for four people to "captain the ship." A lot of partnerships fail due to this structural problem.

We each had our own areas of expertise: Derek's was engineering, Phil's was supply chain and operations, Gary's was sales and marketing, and mine was overall business development. Those are the key building blocks in a start-up. A strong financial or accounting department will come, but it's just not important at the outset.

As the company grew, we knew we wouldn't succeed if someone didn't have overall responsibility for pulling the four of us together. We also needed to have some type of visible structure. Our banker needed to see a defined structure, or he'd picture chaos, and so would our private capital/equity partners. We didn't want our customers to be sitting in meetings wondering who did what. Even our employees would benefit from seeing clearly who held official responsibility for each area of the business.

At the time and still to this day when anyone asks, "How did you become the CEO?" the joke among the partners was always that I had lost the coin toss! But I took on the responsibility of what we called "being the glue" and we kept marching forward.

I'm sure I had a harder time dealing with it than they did, and not because of the extra responsibility; I kind of gravitate to that. It was the burden of having to be the one who had to talk to a partner—who was also either a best friend or my brother—about a challenge or issue. I had to find a way to get comfortable doing it.

I needn't have worried. In the 18 or so years we were together I can count on one hand the number of times I had to end a meeting by saying, "Okay guys, we can't agree on this so we're going to do it this way." My role was to get us in the room and talking about where we wanted to go. We found if we talked problems and ideas out enough, solutions inevitably bubbled up.

The arbitrator on any issue under review came when we asked ourselves two important questions: "Is it good for the customer?" and, "Can we do this profitably?" If the issue or idea didn't pass both, there was no need to get into a disagreement between the partners. With these two simple rules in place, if someone's idea got shot down it was never personal.

There are risks to this approach. Partnerships between friends fall apart all the time—and partners are usually friends first, of course, since you don't go into business with a guy you meet at the bus stop. So when businesses break up, the friendship is almost always severed as well. It's a very dangerous mix. Considering the nature of the personalities and the nature of the business, we are very proud to have stayed in the partnership and made as much money together as we did.

We stuck together for 18 years. People have actually joked that we should write a book on how to do it because we would make more money selling the book to partnerships and entrepreneurs than we ever made building SMTC. After all, we had two brothers and two best friends and it should never have worked.

*   *   *

Still, we had our ups and downs. The company wasn't always profitable. We didn't hit a home run every time. We had other challenges around financing and maintaining working capital after those first six months. We borrowed from banks, got personal lines of credit, and remortgaged our own houses for capital so we could grow. These moves all brought their share of perpetual stress.

About 10 years in, in 1995, we realized that we had to make a decision around growth. SMTC was a one-site operation, doing about $20 million in revenue. While we were proud of what we'd accomplished, we were just making a living and couldn't see a "big score" down the road. Outsourcing was starting to become heavily accepted by the OEMs. It was time to strike. We had to expand.

We started marketing in California and hired a manufacturer's representative. It was a bit of a naive plan: we were hoping to hook up with customers in San Jose and the rest of California to let us build their products 3,000 miles away in Canada. Even though we went to trade shows and met people who liked our business model, they ultimately said, "Too bad you're not located here." The work was never going to come to Toronto.

We had to expand into the United States and open up an operation. Doing business in the United States was a challenging, but appealing idea. It was exciting, and as entrepreneurs we didn't just want to operate a business. We wanted to build something special.

We'd set up from scratch once before, in Toronto, so getting an empty building and buying equipment didn't bother us. People still thought we were just this side of nuts, as here were four Canadians coming into the United States, joining about 150 competitors in the heart of Silicon Valley, and thinking we could do it better. But we did it anyway. We leased an empty building, bought a bunch of equipment, hired people, and started filling up our new San Jose site.

It was an incredibly rewarding experience. When we began years before I can tell you that not one of us pictured ourselves actually setting up internationally. We thought we might do well—maybe even very well—in Canada, but in Silicon Valley? It was not even on our radar. We had to make personal commitments on our mortgages, borrow more money from our bank; we had to re-up. We actually borrowed another few million dollars. It was almost like starting up again. It was a great thrill and a huge business challenge.

In the next five years (1995–2000), we added 10 factories in four countries and 3,000 employees. SMTC went from a $20-million run rate in 1995 to a run rate of about $1 billion. We multiplied our staff by 10. We went from having a single facility to having 10 in 2000. Needless to say, it was something of a rocket ride.

The reasons for our success were a combination of outsourcing gaining prominence and a few lessons we learned about ourselves. For example, we learned after building the San Jose facility from scratch that expanding this way wasn't going to be fast enough. So, in subsequent expansions, we bought companies and integrated their business, employees, and customers into ours. We bought smaller firms at a stage in their growth where their owners were facing big decisions: Should they buy new equipment and grow? Should they pump new money into their business? Or did they want to simply exit the business?

The popularity of outsourcing brought with it a huge tidal wave of opportunity, but it required significant capital investments. It also needed people who were both entrepreneurial and vibrant, because it was going to take another five to 10 years to reap the rewards. Many weren't prepared to wait, which meant there were a number of companies for sale. First we targeted a $5-million business in Texas. Then we went to Charlotte, Ireland, Boston, Denver, Mexico, Wisconsin, and Asia, with the deals getting larger every time.

Ultimately we could not get by on our money and bank financing. We had to start paying for companies with private equity. We ended up with three private equity partners.

Meanwhile, one partner moved south to run the San Jose start-up. We remained a Canadian company, running it from our headquarters in Markham, Ontario. Ultimately we took the company public in July of 2000.

This turned out to be quite fortunate, because we were in a better position than most when disaster struck and the high-tech bubble burst, and as everyone's customers pulled back and started cancelling orders.

So we downsized and reduced our footprint, scaling back to about four facilities and cutting our head count significantly. The company was now returned to a manageable—or I should say appropriate—size.

*   *   *

Around this time I found out that the size of the company isn't as important as staying profitable, efficient, and nimble. One of the surprising but key lessons I learned around this time was to never be afraid of firing a customer. I think a lot of entrepreneurs struggle with this one, but after the high-tech meltdown we had to fire our biggest customer.

It's a tough one to get your head around because you think of all your customers as profitable and worthy, especially in growth mode, but when you go into restructuring mode you have to review everything.

Dell Computer was a $140-million customer and represented 25 per cent of our business, but it was eating up almost all of our working capital and, frankly, it was tough to make a profit from it. I had to go down to Austin, Texas, and fire Dell.

As you can imagine, firing a $140-million customer was a really tough thing to do. It brought strain and stress to our relationship with the board and a tonne of other people just didn't understand. But it had to be done.

For the three years after the high-tech bubble burst, we took the business back into this $300- to $400-million range and made it profitable again, restructuring and rightsizing the business for the new macro economy. As I mentioned, we went public in July 2000, and the meltdown happened that fall, only three months later!

There were a few reasons we had gone public. First, we had private equity partners and, ultimately, they will always look for an exit. We also had the momentum and were one of the last, good private companies available, as most of our competitors had already gone public, and we wanted to reduce our debt.

But soon we came to another fork in the road. After three years of scaling back we wanted to take the company into growth mode again. Not everyone agreed with the strategy. The board members who had already been on our rocket ride and through the gut-wrenching restructuring wanted to review strategic alternatives (sell the business) or stand pat. But to me, in the high-tech business, if you're standing still you're going backwards. Frankly, if our board had decided to sell the business, we were prepared to do it, but staying put wasn't the right way to go. We had constant friction with the board over this and at some point I felt a clear direction was needed again, as that's how SMTC had been built. The partners went ahead and put together a new business plan to move the business forward and when it wasn't accepted by the board, we all left within a year.

Losing control was not easy, but when I left I didn't lose my entrepreneurial spirit. I don't think a true entrepreneur ever does. I became an independent adviser and consultant, and for the past eight years I've been helping businesses restructure their operations and business development areas and, in a couple of cases, actually helping them to sell the business.

Then, in the past year, I did some restructuring and business development work for a company called Artaflex, which is in the exact same industry as SMTC, and I ended up buying the business. I'm not going to tell you that Artaflex is going to earn a billion dollars in revenue. I'm 54 and I'm too old to do that again. That being said, I don't think you ever lose the spark to build something special, especially when others say it can't be done.

That's why when someone tells me my idea is not going to work I always ask them, "How do kites rise?" I tell them, "Kites rise against the wind. You can't get a kite to rise if you're going with the wind." When people tell you something will never work, it means you're going against the wind. If everyone else is doing it you have to do it differently.

On the personal side, you also have to be prepared to listen in business, and that's hard. You've got to be prepared to grow, change, and adapt. Most people are reluctant to change on a personal level, myself included. You have to be able to look at yourself in the mirror and see your shortcomings. And you can't always fix them. Sometimes you have to surround yourself with people with specific strengths. I have always tried to hire people, especially at the senior level, with skill sets equivalent to or superior to mine. Growing a business is very tough, especially if you have managers who don't bring additional skills sets to the table, as everything just falls back on you.

But none of our success would ever have happened without the $50,000 loan my parents gave us to start our little company 26 years ago. Thinking about it brings back a clear memory of a conversation I had with my mother, who passed away a few years ago and who never really had a chance to witness the success of SMTC and the positive impact it had on the lives of the more than 3,000 people we employed.

When we borrowed the money to start SMTC I was married and we had just had the first of two beautiful daughters, Lauren and Krystin. One day I had my six-month-old daughter Lauren sitting on the dining room table, surrounded by family, and my mom called me into the kitchen.

She said to me, "So, what happens if this idea doesn't work?" And I said, "Don't worry; I'll pay you back the $50,000." And I'll never forget this. She said, "I'm not worried about the $50,000." She looked in the dining room at all the sisters, brothers, aunts, and uncles eyeing this little prize on the table and said, "I'm worried about her." I said, "Don't worry, Mom. I'll just go and get a real job."

I can still picture myself saying it to her. To this day I laugh when I think about it, because entrepreneurs who go out and start their business don't consider it a job. It's a passion. In retrospect, telling my mom I had this fallback position, which was supposed to ease her mind, wasn't realistic. Now I know there wasn't a fallback. I was never going to "get a real job." I was always going to be an entrepreneur. It's in my blood.

20
TELL US YOUR STORY

Here is an opportunity to tell your story, now that you have read the others.

FOR ANY ENTREPRENEUR OR BUSINESS OWNER, every day brings a new set of opportunities to explore and challenges to overcome. There is no better way to learn innovative strategies for acting on opportunities and dealing with challenges than hearing how others have already done so. Their lessons learned can save time and aggravation, or even point you in a brand-new direction. This is especially true of business stories demonstrating how ingenuity and determination have broken down barriers to help propel a privately-held business to its next level of success.

Now that you've had the chance to learn from the entrepreneurs featured in this book, here's your opportunity to reciprocate by sharing your own business journey—for possible inclusion in the next edition of *That'll Never Work*.

Visit www.thatllneverwork.ca to share your story. Please include basic logistical information such as the name of your business, industry sector, when and where your company was founded, and its website address. Then, in a minimum of 500 words, tell us your story. What inspired you to become an entrepreneur? What were your early hurdles? Was it tough to convince investors to believe in you and your business idea? As your business matured, what new challenges did you face? What motivates you to keep going today? We know that just as every business is different, each entrepreneur's trials and tribulations are also unique—that's why the sharing of stories and experiences matters.

At KPMG Enterprise™, we also consider ourselves entrepreneurs. KPMG Enterprise was the brainchild of a handful of our partners, who, working with entrepreneurs and mid-sized businesses, felt these business owners wanted something new from their service provider. They required a trusted adviser with a broader business mindset. They needed help tackling a range of business issues beyond accounting and tax. They also wanted to access different areas of expertise at different times, based on their current, and specific, business objectives.

So this group of partners built a business case. Then they convinced both the management committee and the board of KPMG LLP that a new model was appropriate and necessary to help Canadian businesses grow and build shareholder value. This marked the start of KPMG Enterprise, which today has grown to become a national network of professionals dedicated exclusively to working with the business owners and entrepreneurs of Canada's privately-held companies. Over the years, we have grown from this entrepreneurial group of partners into a team of 2,000 professionals, located in 32 locations stretching from Victoria to St. John's. We work with companies in the midst of start-up mode, with many of Canada's largest and most highly regarded private businesses, and with anyone in between. We look forward to learning your story and we wish you continuing success in all of your business ventures.

ACKNOWLEDGEMENTS

While the idea for *That'll Never Work* was inspired by a similar compilation developed by Michael Gaffney and Colin O'Brien, partners at KPMG in Ireland, both of whom bring many years of experience working with private Irish businesses, the Canadian edition quickly took on a life of its own. Elaine Hickey-Dwyer was instrumental in sharing with us their process and experience, ensuring we could design our own launch plan for unearthing great Canadian business leaders with fascinating experiences and stories to share.

This deeply collaborative effort endeavoured to capture the Canadian entrepreneurial spirit and celebrate the inspiring stories of entrepreneurs across the country. The project was endorsed by partners serving the KPMG Enterprise leadership team: Guyle Tippe, Dan Adams, David Adams, Sheldon Jacobs, Tom Zurowski, Brad Klassen, Mary Jo Fedy, Ruth Todd, Denis Trottier, Dennis Fortnum, Pierre Ste. Marie, Beverly Johnson, Todd MacIntosh, Ed Bartucci, Peter Miller, and Bob Young.

On behalf of the KPMG Enterprise leadership team, we would like to recognize and thank all the contributors for their efforts in the development of this book, particularly the collection of entrepreneurial founders and CEOs featured within the chapters, for sharing their stories and supporting the content development process. They were generous with their time, provided thought-provoking viewpoints in line with the overall concept, and were open to sharing their collective experience and wisdom for the benefit of all Canadian entrepreneurs.

We appreciate the experience brought to the project by StrategicAmpersand's Anita Wong and Adam Pletsch, who worked with our entrepreneurs to transform anecdotes and lessons learned into cohesive chapters suited for the printed page. Additionally, we recognize the writing of Mike Martin and Dianne Daniel, and the work of Cindy Watson, Andrew Gouveia, and Claire McCorquodale.

Each featured business story was identified by a KPMG Enterprise professional, so we extend our appreciation to Winston Chui, Dan Adams, Chris Day, Denis Trottier, Peter Miller, Nicolas Pinto, Rajneesh Sapra, Ed Bartucci, Paola D'Agostino, Mark Lang, Gerald Hagerman, Sean Reid, and Jennifer Clement. Project direction was led by Tracy A. Holotuk and coordination was aptly managed by Donna Trifunovic.

Finally, we would like to express our appreciation to Penguin Canada for adeptly steering *That'll Never Work* through the production process and for their collective commitment to editorial excellence: Andrea Magyar, Mary Ann Blair, Chrystal Kocher, and David Whiteside.

PHOTO CREDITS

Page 3, Toni Canale-Parola, KPMG Enterprise

Page 5, Gina Becker

Page 15, Alex Neil / Liz Potter

Page 25, Wellington West Holdings Inc.

Page 35, James Ingram

Page 47, Brenda Wallace

Page 57, Factory Optical / Optiks International

Page 69, Don Miller

Page 81, C & N Photography

Page 93, Joe Clauss

Page 103, Royal LePage, Your Community Realty – Marketing Department

Page 109, Courtesy Turtle Island Recycling

Page 121, Pam Toem, Great Takes Photography

Page 129, Carolyn Wyatt

Page 141, Emerge Learning

Page 149, Emily Stover, Nulogy Corporation

Page 157, Stéven Talbot, Productions RÉSÖ Inc.

Page 165, Teri Price

Page 177, Courtesy Easton's Group of Hotels Inc.

Page 187, Paul Walker